Praise for *Strategy*

'*Strategy Sprints* offers methods for not o[nly]
also enjoying your life more by helping you focus on what matters most.' …
EYAL, AUTHOR OF *HOOKED* AND *INDISTRACTABLE*

'Ready to IGNITE your sales? Then the Strategy Sprints method is for you! Following Simon Severino's blueprint will ensure your company becomes ON FIRE.' JOHN LEE DUMAS, HOST OF *ENTREPRENEURS ON FIRE* PODCAST AND AUTHOR OF *THE COMMON PATH TO UNCOMMON SUCCESS*

'What Simon Severino offers is rare in this world. His curiosity and affection for humanity shine through this book and the Strategy Sprints method he shares in it.' PETER BLOCK, AUTHOR OF *FLAWLESS CONSULTING* AND *THE ABUNDANT COMMUNITY*

'Your sales will soar with the Strategy Sprints method. This book has all the marketing, sales and operations blueprints needed to run an agile company.' DAVID HENZEL, CEO, UPCOACH

'Business is strategy and the Strategy Sprints method gives businesses a systematic way to identify and implement strategies to reach your most important goals. Practical and doable, it is a must-read.' PAUL J ZAK, FOUNDER, IMMERSION NEUROSCIENCE

'This book is packed with wisdom, insights and practical tools to help take your business to the next level. It will equip you with the game plan to make the impact you want to have with your business.' SIMON ALEXANDER ONG, AWARD-WINNING LIFE COACH AND AUTHOR OF *ENERGIZE*

'The Strategy Sprints method is what CEOs need today to rise to the moment. Clear, concise and compelling.' JOHN LIVESAY, GLOBAL SPEAKER ON SALES AND STORYTELLING

'If you're an entrepreneur or business leader, you need to read *Strategy Sprints*. It's more than a book – it's a complete roadmap for business acceleration. So study it… and soar!' DANNY INY, CEO, MIRASEE AND AUTHOR OF *TEACH YOUR GIFT* AND *EFFORTLESS*

'Being a CEO can be overwhelming. Simon Severino's approach in this book breaks it down so you can feel confident as a leader and create a successful business! No matter what level you're at in your business, Severino points out exactly what chapters to focus on for the biggest impact and immediate results. I've already applied some of the strategies I've learned and am excited to keep strengthening my business using his wisdom!' MELINDA COHAN, CEO, THE COACHES CONSOLE AND AUTHOR OF THE CONFIDENT COACH

'I love the value and heart-centered quality that Simon Severino brings to his work and to this book. A must-read for anyone how wants to scale fast.' CHRISTINE SCHLONSKI, FOUNDER, HEART SELLS! ACADEMY

'*Strategy Sprints* is the book entrepreneurs have been waiting for. It provides practical strategies to master marketing, sales and operations in an agile way.' SABRI ERYIGIT, MANAGING PARTNER, NEXT ACTION PARTNERS

'*Strategy Sprints* makes it easy to see where your business can change to grow fast, and easy to see how to make the needed changes. It's all about becoming the CEO, and Simon Severino points the way.' JOHN JONAS, CEO, ONLINEJOBS.PH

'This is an inspiring must-read for everybody involved in a SaaS or internet-based service business. Simon Severino offers a tour d'horizon through 12 of the most crucial success drivers for these types of endeavours. His key message across all the 12 topics is as wise as it is clear: focus.' MARKUS ORENGO, OWNER, SOCIAL SYSTEMS ENGINEERING

'There are a gazillion business books out there. In a world with too much noise, few of them give you only the essentials. Fewer still inspire you to act on those essentials. Read Simon Severino's *Strategy Sprints*.' DAN KING, CO-FOUNDER, FIRESIDE STRATEGIC

'The book provides concrete and actionable guidance for people and organizations that want to grow fast.' LUKAS ZENK, PROFESSOR FOR INNOVATION AND NETWORK RESEARCH, DONAU-UNIVERSITÄT KREMS, AUSTRIA

'If you want to grow a business fast, then reading *Strategy Sprints* will support you to get there. When Simon Severino shows a business owner what to focus on, and what *not* to focus on, they can double their revenue in 90 days.' RENNIE GABRIEL, AUTHOR OF WEALTH ON ANY INCOME

'Simon Severino's book is a literal manifestation of its title, that is, a strategy SPRINT that will get you from here to there in record time… and enjoy doing so! With help from easy-to-follow lists, fun graphics, useful tools and ongoing advice, this book is a kind of entrepreneurial growth manual. By all means, immerse yourself in this book! It will move you ahead with all due deliberate speed… and momentum!' KEN LIZOTTE CMC, AUTHOR OF *THE EXPERT'S EDGE*

'*Strategy Sprints* nails all the elements a marketer must master to succeed in today's hugely crowded marketplace in order to profit and thrive.' JACKIE LAPIN, FOUNDER, SPEAKERTUNITY®, THE SPEAKER AND LEADER RESOURCE COMPANY

'*Strategy Sprints* brings simplicity and efficiency for immediate impact and results on your business development. A practical backbone to get things done with agility and consistency. Warmly recommended.' CYRIL LEGRAND, CEO, OXFORD LEADERSHIP

'*Strategy Sprints* is brilliant for the builders and creators – people everywhere striving to build their dream and create meaningful impact through their business. It's the map to streamline your business, speed your growth and avoid some of the painful missteps that are so common in the business building journey. An absolute must-read!' HEATHER PEARCE CAMPBELL, ATTORNEY AND LEGAL COACH, THE LEGAL WEBSITE WARRIOR®

'If you've been looking for the missing owner's manual for a successful online business, *Strategy Sprints* is it. Nothing is assumed and nothing is left out. Simon gives you literally *everything* you need to launch, grow, and scale a business. This book is so good, I wish I had written it. A generous goldmine of smart, actionable advice.' DAVID NEWMAN, CSP, AUTHOR OF *DO IT! MARKETING* AND *DO IT! SPEAKING*

'Simon Severino presents his lessons and learnings in an authentic and entertaining way. By experiencing and sharing what most Entrepreneurs will go through, through his own lens, he manages to weave an entertaining, highly educational and comprehensive learning experience. A must-read for any aspiring or growing entrepreneur!' JAMES LAM, FOUNDER, LOOK AHEAD MARKETING

Strategy Sprints

12 ways to accelerate growth for an agile business

Simon Severino

Publisher's note
Every possible effort has been made to ensure that the information contained in this book is accurate at the time of going to press, and the publishers and author cannot accept responsibility for any errors or omissions, however caused. No responsibility for loss or damage occasioned to any person acting, or refraining from action, as a result of the material in this publication can be accepted by the editor, the publisher or the author.

First published in Great Britain and the United States in 2022 by Kogan Page Limited

Apart from any fair dealing for the purposes of research or private study, or criticism or review, as permitted under the Copyright, Designs and Patents Act 1988, this publication may only be reproduced, stored or transmitted, in any form or by any means, with the prior permission in writing of the publishers, or in the case of reprographic reproduction in accordance with the terms and licences issued by the CLA. Enquiries concerning reproduction outside these terms should be sent to the publishers at the undermentioned addresses:

2nd Floor, 45 Gee Street	8 W 38th Street, Suite 902	4737/23 Ansari Road
London	New York, NY 10018	Daryaganj
EC1V 3RS	USA	New Delhi 110002
United Kingdom		India

www.koganpage.com

Kogan Page books are printed on paper from sustainable forests.

© Simon Severino, 2022

The right of Simon Severino to be identified as the author of this work has been asserted by him in accordance with the Copyright, Designs and Patents Act 1988.

Strategy Sprints is a registered trademark.

ISBNs
Hardback   978 1 3986 0351 6
Paperback   978 1 3986 0349 3
Ebook   978 1 3986 0350 9

British Library Cataloguing-in-Publication Data
A CIP record for this book is available from the British Library.

Library of Congress Cataloging-in-Publication Number
2021950064

Typeset by Integra Software Services, Pondicherry
Print production managed by Jellyfish
Printed and bound by CPI Group (UK) Ltd, Croydon, CR0 4YY

For all Sprinters,
the people who build something bigger than themselves.
Who shift from star to galaxy.
Keep rolling.

Contents

About the author xiii
Foreword xv
Read this first xvii
Become a Strategy Sprints coach xix

Introduction 1

01 Eliminate the competition 7
    Step 1: Are you vanilla? 9
    Step 2: Define your business 10
    Step 3: Determine who you serve 11
    Step 4: Embody your vision 16
    Your vision in three years 18
    Final thoughts 20

02 Nail your message and your brand 21
    Step 1: Define the hero and the mission 23
    Step 2: Pick one villain and have a plan to beat them 24
    Step 3: Call to action 28
    Step 4: Describe success 29
    Step 5: Summarize the hero's transformation 30
    Final thoughts 31

03 Your growth plan 33
    Four growth levers 34
    Lever #1: Price and packaging 34
    Lever #2: Sales time and sales rate 35
    Lever #3: Systematizing 36
    Lever #4: Exponential productivity 37
    90-day growth plan 38
    Final thoughts 46

04 Real-time decision making with the Strategy Sprints method 47
    CEO reality 47
    The Strategy Sprints Compass 50
    Daily habits 53
    Weekly habits 56
    Monthly habits 57
    Final thoughts 59

05 Daily flow 61
    The project list 63
    The daily flow 66
    The protection systems 70
    Final thoughts 72

06 Find traction instead of distraction in your ideal week 73
    Step 1: Map your ideal week 75
    Step 2: Create traction in your business 77
    Step 3: Add time blockers to your calendar 78
    Step 4: Respect your personal energy patterns 80
    Final thoughts 82

07 Value ladder 83
    Define your main product 85
    Describe the sample 87
    Know your winning channels 88
    Have a main upsell 89
    Include a continuity offer 90
    The 80% ready page 91
    Final thoughts 93

08 Predictable sales and reaching people more 95
    Sales tracker 97
    Sales estimation numbers 98
    Scripts for discovery calls 99
    Ten must-haves of an effective sales script 102
    Seven stages of customer relationship management 105
    The art of the follow-up 111
    Final thoughts 112

09 Feedback is the breakfast of champions 113
    Understand what your clients really need 115
    Calculate feedback the Strategy Sprints way 117
    Win big with your feedback 119
    Final thoughts 119

10 The seven elements of marketing 121
    1. Positioning 122
    2. Traction channels 123
    3. Reusable content pieces 124
    4. Email automation 126
    5. Retargeting ads (FB/IG) 130
    6. Unique mechanism 130
    7. Irresistible offer 131
    Final thoughts 132

11 Your assets 135
    The 30-second pitch 136
    The 7-second tagline 137
    Your uniqueness 138
    Your own phrase 139
    Social proof 140
    Authority content 141
    Professional platform 142
    Final thoughts 143

12 Hiring system overview 145
    Create the job scorecard 147
    Write the standard operating procedures 150
    Build an inspiring landing page and application 151
    Final thoughts 154

13 Hiring simplified 157
    Social outreach with hiring copy 159
    Three tests 161
    Interviews 164
    Trial, offer, or rejection 166

Hiring system checklist 167
Final thoughts 168

Appendix 1: A note to you, the reader 171
Appendix 2: YOUR GAME PLAN 173
Index 175

About the author

Simon Severino is an author, CEO of Strategy Sprints and host of the Strategy Sprints podcast.

He has interviewed powerhouse entrepreneurs like Rita McGrath, David Allen, Nir Eyal, Perry Marshall, Verne Harnish, Brian Kurtz and hundreds more on business, productivity and growth.

He helps business owners in SaaS and Services run their companies more effectively, resulting in sales that soar. He created the Strategy Sprints™ method that doubles revenue in 90 days by getting owners out of the weeds. Simon leads a global team of Certified Strategy Sprints™ Coaches who help clients gain market share and work in weekly sprints, which results in fast execution.

As a member of SVBS (Silicon Valley Blockchain Society) he enables cross-stage capital flows and helps minimize execution risks in technology start-ups.

His team is trusted by Google, Consilience Ventures, Roche, Amgen, AbbVie and hundreds of frontier teams. He is a TEDx speaker, and has appeared on over 500 podcasts. He writes for *Forbes* and *Entrepreneur* magazine about scaling digital businesses.

Foreword

When Simon Severino asked me to join him on his podcast to discuss my book, *The Lost Art of Closing*, we became fast friends. We stayed on the video conference for over 45 minutes after recording, the conversation turning to his work at Strategy Sprints. As our conversation continued, so did my interest in his business. My businesses were all doing well, but like a lot of entrepreneurs, the largest part of our strategy was 'grinding out the work'. At the end of our call, Simon and I agreed to discuss me joining his programme (and it is a programme).

Simon is well read, and he is a student. Simon continually searches for the best strategies and tactics, but what he provides in Strategy Sprints, both the programme and this book, is a disciplined process for growing your business faster – and with greater control. One obligation of a writer is to speak the truth, and because I am writing this Foreword, I owe you, the reader, the full and unvarnished truth, as one who has done the work under Simon's guidance.

Simon and his team required me to do the work to position my company for greater growth. You know how you recognize the problems in your business? You know how you spend all of your time working in the business and not on the business? Well, Strategy Sprints will provide you with sprints that will have you address every area of your business. Some of the sprints will reveal problems you have left unaddressed. But know that at the end of each sprint, you will feel so much better about your company and your work. From sprint to sprint, you will gain a sense of control and certainty that gives you the confidence to grow, knowing you have the processes in place to support the acceleration of your company.

I am a very good salesperson and sales leader, but what I am not is a marketer. The work I did with Simon and his team started me on a journey to professionalize my marketing, starting with capturing all the key metrics I had ignored. Simon's book recommendations also provided me support on my journey. My team now has scorecards and documented processes in place, making it easier and faster to bring new people into the company, each knowing what's expected of them and how best to produce results.

Here is my best advice to you: don't read this book as if it is a book. Instead, do the work one chapter at a time. Spending a week on each area in the book will improve your business – and it will improve your life outside of work by giving you the confidence your business is growing with you working fewer hours in the business and a few more on the business.

Do Good Work.

Anthony Iannarino
Author of *Elite Sales Strategies: A Guide to Being One-Up, Creating Value, and Becoming Truly Consultative*

Read this first

Just to say thank you for reading my book, I'd love to share the tools and templates I refer to in this book at no cost whatsoever – it's my gift to you.

ACTION TOOLS

strategysprints.com/tools

Become a Strategy Sprints coach
Get paid to help people close the gap between dreaming and doing

Learn more: strategysprints.com/certification

Introduction

A note to you

My mission in life is to help Sprinters realize their dreams. Sprinters are the people who build and do – more than they talk. The creators. Being a creator is lonely. And risky. So, in this book, if you'll allow me, I take on the posture of your coach, not your critic. I'm the truth-teller who's rooting for you. I am here to sing your song, with you, until you know the words by heart.

Why? You have people who look up to you. Who depend on you. The way you live your life shapes the way other people live theirs. If you are free and powerful, others will give themselves more permission to be free and powerful.

I'm the CEO of a consulting company and have overseen well over 10,000 executive teams executing go-to-market strategies. You will meet many of them later on in this book. And from CEO to CEO, let me be honest. Only a few of us will be around long term. Are you ready to be one of the ones that make it?

With freedom comes responsibility. You can never have one without the other.

My story

I generated half a million euros in revenue the first year I started my business, Strategy Sprints. When I tell this story, people commonly say, 'Wow, you must have been so happy!' But I didn't feel happy. In fact, I was miserable because I was working all the time. Not seeing my wife enough. Mostly on planes. All the cities started to look the same. Airports looked the same. Hotels looked the same.

At that point, I couldn't see how to do less work without hurting revenue. While fulfilling the work, I had no time to generate leads or close sales. Also, my cash flow volatility was too high. The sales went up and down in huge waves, keeping me awake at night.

Then, my wife became pregnant, and I had to create a smarter business model. This was ironic because I built Strategy Sprints so 'work can feel like friends playing basket', to guide business owners to create meaningful work that does not feel like work. Somehow, in doing so for others, I forgot to do the same for myself. In seeking to make my work more fun, I realized I didn't know *where* my business was or what path we were on. This is a common problem for frantically busy CEOs not growing; you don't know how to or if you're ready to scale, what investments make sense, etc.

CEO reality

My wake-up call was this: no MBA prepares you for the dozens of decisions you have to make as a business owner every day. When your team brings problems and ideas to you, you're expected to know the answer to:

- 'Should we offer a lower-priced product for that sub-audience?'
- 'Which key role do we hire next?'
- 'Should we run paid ads?'
- 'What kind of content should we be creating?'

Seems straightforward enough, yet after working with thousands of business owners, I know that most of them lack the data required to make such decisions, just as I once did.

Not to mention, where are we taught how to create systems to process all those projects and ideas? We often turn to models that create cultures in a business that fail the stakeholders. When an issue needs a resolution, the team might be free to say, 'We can't do that now. It's not on the agenda!' Or 'That's not in my job description.' And even worse, 'I did something about the problem. I put it on a to-do list for someone else.' If those attitudes and lack of ownership for key tasks are present in your business, there's a better way.

To know where I was in my business so I could reshape it, I turned to my own Strategy Sprints method to change my habits. I wanted to recreate my business based on an ethos that you can take any complex issue and bring it down to its simplest parts – a minimalist approach. Not only does my business thrive with this freedom, but my clients do, too. In fact, today hundreds of business owners in 114 countries use and love my Strategy Sprints too. Experienced management consultants get certified in the Strategy Sprints method to use these habits with their clients. And in this book, you will read all about our most successful strategies that work for us and our clients.

How to read this book

As your business grows and evolves, you'll return to specific chapters to brush up on that aspect of growing and scaling your business. In many of the chapters, I also refer to additional templates, tools, and resources available on my website. You will find that link at the end of every chapter and may want to bookmark it for easy reference. Do take advantage of those bonus materials to get the most out of this book.

Use *Strategy Sprints* to create the freedom and sales you want in your business. In deciding where your business is now and where you want it to grow next, I find it helpful to consider my Five Levels of Business Fitness. Each level is covered in this book and reflects the appropriateness of different tactics and tools. Being a Level One doesn't mean you have a low score, but it does mean different strategies will work best to get you to a Level Two, and if you try to skip to a strategy for Level Five, you're likely to waste time and money on an idea that wasn't right for you. I don't want that to happen, so review this list of five levels of marketing to identify where your business is now and the next step that's right for your growth. I cover all these strategies at different points in this book.

Level One

If you are a Level One business, you will have several offers and an unclear tiering for prices. It may also be unclear who the target customer is or what problem your offer solves if you even do have a website. All your processes are manual. Many businesses are at this stage. If they spend one dollar in advertising, they waste one dollar. They waste a lot of time. That's why marketing and authority content don't work at this level. Get clear on your one avatar (Chapter 1) and Main Offer (Chapter 7). Then, put them together on your website (Chapter 2).

Level Two

If you have a website that clearly states one offer for one customer at one price then you are at Level Two. You also have a social media presence where you show up regularly. With a full Value Ladder, the next step is not to start scaling. You think you're ready because your branding is in place, but now is the time to improve your automation (see Chapter 10) and sales (see Chapter 8).

Level Three

At Level Three, you have a CRM in place where every single stage of your customer's journey has at least one email template that is automated to move leads through your Value Ladder. This is how you scale, by turning warm leads into hot ones in a way that doesn't require manual tasks or being in person. You also have a high rate of conversion on those hot leads, so your sales process is effective. This is the point at which it makes sense to create a mix of organic and paid marketing (Chapter 10) as well as hire for key roles in sales and operations (Chapter 4 and Chapter 12).

Level Four

If you are spending $1 in paid advertisement and making $3 to $4 in return, then you are scaling and growing your business. You consistently generate sales calls and have a team that follows your sales process to close them. You also have a delivery team in operations to fulfil the sales and manage the customer experiences. Now you want to continue putting money into your best marketing channels and building your team to support more customers. Put a growth plan in place (Chapter 3) and make sure your customers are happy by asking them and listening (Chapter 10).

Level Five

Congratulations. You have a full circle in which the business is fun to run and your profits are healthy. Now you are scaling, and your return to your ad spend will increase because you reuse the leads who don't buy from you and move them back into your direct marketing system for another offer. This is what I mean by a full circle. Even the people who don't buy from you are now in your relationship-building sequence. You warm up all the leads in a continuous fashion. That's when your business is an effortless, well-oiled machine.

At Level Five, you have a business that works even when you are on holiday or take a long summer. You're not the business operator. You're the CEO. Continue optimizing and refining your business (Chapter 5) and defining your freedom (Chapter 6).

Not sure what your business's fitness level is today? I invite you to take the Your Game Plan Audit. The Your Game Plan Audit takes just a few minutes to complete and is the first step for helping you discover how to:

- react faster to surprising events;
- reduce risk;
- leverage your unique strengths;
- increase momentum;
- double your sales.

Visit strategysprints.com to take the free assessment and receive your game plan report.

Whatever level your business falls into now, let's get you to the next level, starting with your positioning in Chapter 1.

CHAPTER ONE

Eliminate the competition

In 2019 I was asked to give a TEDx talk, which I called 'Be a Category of One'. In that talk, I share a story about playing football as a kid in Italy. At one game, our head coach called out to me, 'Go, Simon! Shoot the ball! Score!'

He would push me to score, and I would freeze. I was afraid of moving. I was afraid of attacking. I was afraid of winning. All I could think of was to flee or hide because fear was crippling inside of me. Images of what-ifs kept flashing through my mind. And those same thoughts stopped me from doing what I had to do to win the game. It felt safer for me to stay with the pack instead of pulling ahead and going for the score. In other words, I was being 'vanilla'.

Vanilla is no way to be a successful athlete, and it doesn't work for success in business or any other area of life, either. We try to stand out and be incomparable to our competitors because our business will die a natural death if we don't. In fact, most businesses fail. There are a lot of reasons why businesses fail, but one of the most common is failing to be different from competitors.

In my consulting business, Strategy Sprints, I have worked with many business owners who thought their businesses were stagnating or even failing because they couldn't keep up with their industries. As we would dig deeper into their issues, we'd never fail to uncover untested ideas and unique purposes that they never implemented because of fear of going against the grain, of being un-vanilla. But, when we zig when everyone else is zagging, that's how to score points in football, and the same is true in business.

When you take a risk to stand out and be different, the outcome is often not as bad as you think it will be. In fact, most of the time, it's quite the opposite. You're revealing your primary strategic advantage so that your best clients clearly see you're the only option to solve their problem. Standing out from your competition gives you power to:

- influence others by being who you are;
- operate from a foundation based on your definition of genuine purpose; and
- work from a position of confidence in relation to the impact you can make in people's lives.

If you let others define your work, your business becomes vanilla. It becomes like everyone else's work. Your uniqueness? Gone. To create something remarkable and relevant, inoculate against the wishes of the outside world. You have to protect your genius and stop hiding behind what's culturally expected. Because most of the time, society's accepted way of doing things may not be helpful for you to stand out from the competition.

Do you have competition? If yes, there is a real need in the marketplace for what you are offering, and that's good news. But it will be difficult for you to make profits in that market because you will always be compared, and that will drive prices down, which eats up your profit margins. In today's competitive landscape, it's not enough to be great. You also have to be unique. This is challenging in a competitive field with established norms. Chan Kim and Renee Mauborgne address this problem in their 2015 book *Blue Ocean Strategy*, in which they describe a red ocean as the space where cutthroat competitors fight over the same audience, turning the waters bloody red.

The water turns red for businesses that do what is expected and copy behaviours from others, leading to everyone doing the same thing, which limits an industry to its 'best practice'. But the thing is, the industry best practice is something somebody developed and was at one time unique. And you can also come up with better ways and ideas that go against what's usual. Kim and Mauborgne refer to this as the *blue ocean*, where you are a category of one. There, all competition becomes irrelevant.

In this chapter I share with you my four steps to help businesses stop being vanilla and break through the noise to be a category of one. In the discussion, I'll refer to an example from a colleague of mine who's a positioning strategist, and their project with a tech start-up. The four steps are:

Step 1: Determine, are you vanilla?
Step 2: Decide what business you are in so you can be incomparable.
Step 3: Pinpoint who you serve and why you're their only option.
Step 4: Know your short- and long-term visions.

When you follow these steps, you can answer the most important questions for your positioning: *What makes you stand out?* And *who is your offer for?*

Step 1: Are you vanilla?

The tech start-up my colleague consulted with for positioning strategy sold for over US $1 billion, but before that could happen, they had to get positioning right. They'd had some hiccups, like when they first tried selling their software directly to consumers. Free versions that were just as good quickly destroyed that potential sales model. The next hope was to pivot to large enterprises as their ideal clients. They knew that to be successful with that model, they needed help with the messaging.

They had a team of sales reps calling large enterprises to offer their products and services, but the problem was, they were all having a hard time closing sales. Week after week, they made sales presentations following excellent pitch decks on the benefits and features of their offer. And at the end of each pitch, the client had the same remark every time: 'Why shouldn't I use your competitor?' To which the salespeople would mumble a weak answer in return, unable to address the objection. The competitor was the market leader, and all prospective client conversations ended here, where they'd essentially sold the competition. One sales rep after the other was fired.

While this story appears to tell a tale of failure to anticipate marketplace innovations or to hire qualified salespeople, I argue there's more going on beneath the surface. As the start-up was finding its footing, they were trying to figure out who they were like, instead of where they were different. In other words, they were playing safe and vanilla, making boring choices that aligned with their industry's standards. If you struggle to make sales and struggle to overcome objections and explain how your offer is different from others, your business may have a vanilla problem, too. Imagine if you could create your own completely unique industry and create all your own rules. You can.

The most successful businesses defy the limits of 'industry'. In what industry does Apple operate? Siemens? Tesla? The leaders of those companies show their uniqueness instead of making excuses, and this tech company needed to do the same.

Step 2: Define your business

The start-up hit a bit of luck in the salesperson hiring process, finally. A sales rep candidate came in for an interview and was asked, 'Why should we hire you?'

The candidate replied, 'I tell you why, because my buddy is the head of investment at a huge, global shipping company.' He got the job and then delivered his first pitch in a meeting with the positioning strategist and the head of logistics at that company.

The client asked for a specific feature the salesperson was able to quickly demonstrate. What happened next was extraordinary. The client became so excited, he physically jumped up and down, then ran to call his colleagues into the meeting. As a result, the deal closed. The same question came up at the next meeting with another global shipping company. Sales started kicking in. The positioning strategist now realized a trend and wondered: *Should we reposition ourselves from enterprise software to global shipping software?* This question gets to the heart of Step 2. In defining your business, the goal is to find an uncrowded space of open-wide growth potential. Previously, the start-up had defined themselves by their product, but at this point, they considered instead defining themselves by their best customers.

You become a category of one when you define your business in contrast to the competition, instead of alongside them. Consider if clients don't buy your services or products, where else would they go? It is important to know who others might compare you to, so you can get to the heart of what makes you unique. In my business, we collate this data with our Equalizer Spreadsheet, which I give you a link to at the end of this chapter. You can see an example of how it will look with sample inputs in Figure 1.1.

The goal of the Equalizer Spreadsheet is to look at the different tools and methods of delivery others in your industry are using, like AI, Data-Driven Dashboards, Integrations, etc. Also make a list of the benefits of your offer and the competitors. Then, you can grade your performance from 1–10 based on where you're winning (7–10), where you're 'meh' (4–6), and where you're losing (1–3). For example, if one of the benefits is 'speed', you'll rate your business's status on speed. If you're majorly focused on speed, that's a 10. If you're weak on speed, that's a 1. The idea is to gauge your current business's standing based on the benefits that make clients buy from you and rate your competitors in comparison.

With your chosen criteria and ratings, then create three buckets for your weakest, 'okay', and strongest areas. This will show you what offers or

FIGURE 1.1 The Equalizer Spreadsheet

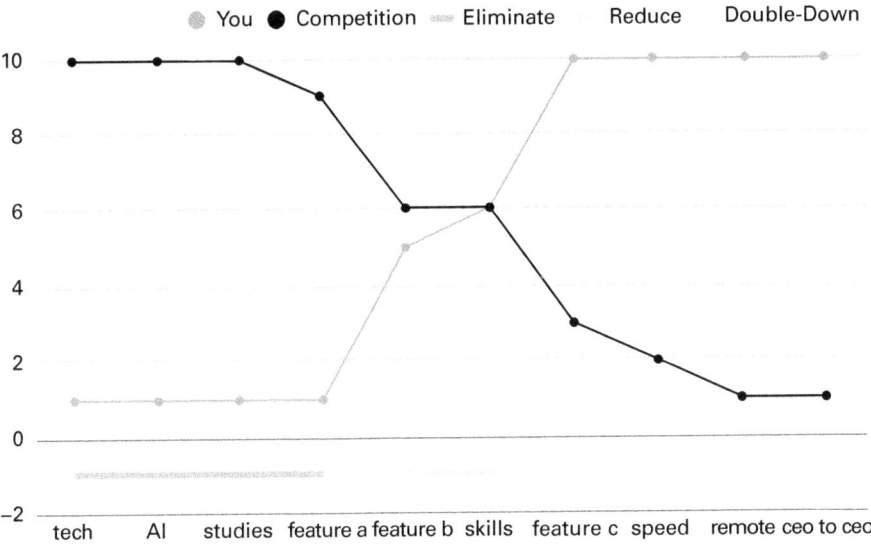

services to eliminate (weakest), reduce (okay), or double down on (strongest). Where you decide to double down, that becomes your definition and the basis by which you stand out as the only competition for your unique offer.

You're ready to define your business when you know what you are #1 on, which makes you unique. For instance, in my business we have 17 courses on strategy and growth but decided not to sell them. We did that because in this analysis for ourselves, we found that our differentiator – where we stand out in the marketplace – is the business of transformation, not education. In the short term, we may lose some revenue by not selling those assets, but we stay true to our definition.

Step 3: Determine who you serve

As the start-up in our example was deciding to reposition from the enterprise niche to the global shipping niche, the logical answer was, 'No way. The shipping market is too small.' However, the alternative to repositioning themselves in the marketplace was staying in the price battle with the competitor, who was bigger by far and couldn't be beaten on price. They brainstormed the ideal scenarios and how it would affect their business.

In the end, they made the shift that was transformational for the business. They swam free from competition. And something amazing happened when they went all-in on being a global shipping software: instead of having to reach out to shipping firms, those groups were picking up the phone to call the tech start-up. This is what I meant earlier about zigging where others zag.

> *You don't need hundreds of clients.*
> *You need one client, hundreds of times.*

'The only kind of writing is rewriting.'
ERNEST HEMINGWAY, *A MOVEABLE FEAST*

I often think about Hemingway's approach to writing because it mirrors my approach to business. In essence, he says the act of writing itself is rewriting what you have already rewritten. Business positioning is the same. When you don't grasp this principle, you might repeatedly try to reinvent from scratch and work your marketing team overtime when instead you could simply innovate.

After all, you know who your ideal client is. You just need to write it down, act accordingly every week, measure your results, and continue to refine. After many refinements or rewriting, the ideal client becomes defined and simply articulated, with the precision of Hemingway. And by the way, he edited the last page of *A Farewell to Arms* a stunning 39 times. How many times have you revised your ideal client? Not that many times, I bet.

Like Hemingway, the positioning strategist went through hundreds of iterations of who the start-up's ideal client was, and during their tenure the company grew in revenue from just a few million dollars to nearly 20 million. When they left, the start-up sold for around a billion dollars. Why? Because they kept refining and got their positioning right. How? By pitching to hundreds of prospects and using the collected feedback to narrow down their ideal client as precisely as possible.

When we coach business owners with the Strategy Sprints method, we pick three goals and three numbers. And these numbers get measured and refined every seven days for 12 consecutive weeks. That creates the habit of refinement; that brings the 'Hemingway' out of every CEO, as I discuss in more detail in Chapter 4.

Going narrow with your audience is scary, but crucial to deliver big results. One of the biggest mistakes I see every day is audience targeting, but done badly. Often, when businesses define their ideal client they write down demographics (Age, Gender, Location, Job Role) and forget to define the deeper self (Dreams, Goals, Beliefs, Needs). Here's an example. Guess who this person is…

1 Age +65
2 Father
3 Married twice
4 Born in England
5 Dog lover
6 High Net Worth Individual

From that description, who do you imagine? If you said Prince Charles, that's right. If you said Ozzy Osbourne, that's also right. The damage is clear: in the description, you have not understood either of them. The offer that Ozzy Osbourne will find appealing will be probably not the right one for Prince Charles. Demographics are just the surface. You have to go deeper.

Beginners make this mistake all the time, thinking that the biggest market is the best way to start. Unfortunately, some strategy consultants also believe the same thing. But the best market entry is narrow, and once you dominate that one specific market, expansion to adjacent markets comes easy. For instance, notice my description of the Strategy Sprints team coaches:

1 Business owners
2 39 years old
3 Hate commuting
4 Want to spend the mornings and evenings with their two kids (two and five years old)
5 Their friends say they work too much
6 Ambition to scale their business
7 But just working more is not an option
8 They have to fire themselves from fulfilment
9 They have a passion to create a business capable of running itself

Not only is this list longer than the previous list, but it's far more specific. This is the level at which you should know your ideal client so you can create the right messaging to show them that you have no competition and that you understand them better than anyone else. Maybe even better than they understand themselves.

$1.3 million annual revenue at age 26

A masterful example of effective audience targeting is Ali Abdaal. He has a deep understanding of his audience, and consistently delivers value to them. Aged 26, he has made $1.3 million in revenue from YouTube; 2.3 million people have subscribed to his YouTube channel and clicked through his affiliate links.

When he started, Ali Abdaal had no clue who his ideal client was and what they needed. So he thought, 'How can I just give value to the people around me?' These were medical students like him. Slowly, he picked up more information about them, and bit by bit, his clarity emerged.

He describes his ideal avatar as:

1. Male
2. 20–21 years old
3. Asian
4. Living in London
5. Studying medicine
6. Named something like 'Ali' or 'Mohammed'
7. Prefers board games to discos
8. Has Asian parents constantly remarking to work harder
9. Really likes reading self-help books
10. Wants to start a YouTube channel

Note that he went many levels deep in segmenting his audience. Knowing whom he served quite well, he launched many free courses on Skillshare on how to edit videos for YouTube. That enterprise built his first audience.

In 2020, when he launched his course, PTYA: Part-Time YouTuber Academy, we discussed pricing. This is how I recall our conversation going:

Ali: 'What if nobody buys it? I am afraid nobody will show up.'
Simon: 'What is your estimation?'
Ali: 'I hope at least 15 will buy.'

Confidence is an issue even for elite performers like Ali, as he estimated 15 buyers when the real number of customers he actually converted was 350. If you want to dig deeper into the techniques elite coaches use every day to raise confidence in athletes, I recommend *How Champions Think* (2016) by Bob Rotella.

Ali: 'Is it really ok to ask them for money? ... I don't know, does the course really create the amount of value to justify the price?'

Launch day came. 350 students enrolled in the first cohort. Ali's revenue for this debut cohort was $273,000.

The second cohort in 2021 launched with a max limit of 200 students at double the price. Ali's revenue for cohort two was $400,000.

As you can see in Ali's case, if we get positioning right, the money will follow. The reason Ali has huge impact is that he got positioning right and shows up every day to offer value to his audience.

Okay, are you ready to do this for yourself? There is a method to get around demographics and into your best customer's heart and mind. Here's a list of questions to ask yourself that get nine layers deep.

1. Who is your ideal client?
2. What are their dreams?
3. Their aspirations?
4. What keeps them awake at night?
5. What are their beliefs?
6. What do they hate most?
7. Which problems do they need to solve?
8. Who do they want to impress?
9. Who is around them, expecting something from them?

> Want to coach with me like Ali? I invite you to try one FREE week of coaching in my high-level Strategy Sprints community. The link to join is on my Strategy Sprints home page, www.strategysprints.com.

As you answer the questions, be as specific and descriptive as possible, as if you're telling a driver whom to look for to pick up at the airport or setting them up for a business meeting.

Step 4: Embody your vision

Once the start-up in our example went all-in on being the global shipping software solution, their next client conversations went very differently. If a client asked, 'What about the competitor?', the start-up's salespeople had the perfect answer every time: 'They are the best generalist for their perfect customers, but the thing is, you are a global shipping company. We are *the* software for global shipping!' The more they said it, the more they believed this vision of who they were, and they quickly became the software for global shipping, essentially speaking that vision into reality.

The positioning strategist led this tech start-up from dreaming, wishing, and hoping to get out from under the thumb of a competitor to completely redefining themselves and threatening the bigger business, which led to a lucrative buy-out. This was not achieved with a mission statement, which you can find a lot of other business books telling you to write about now. I'm not telling you to do that because mission statements don't work. They're a fantasyland. A mere piece of paper. They don't work because in the moment when you need them, they will not be right there in your body to help you make the right decision.

For example, you craft a mission statement about you finishing your first marathon: 'I want to be as fit as when I was 16 years old.' Put that piece of paper on the wall. Enrol into a gym membership. For the first month you run daily, then decrease your frequency and finally stop training at all. Your confidence goes down, and you'll find a rational reason to give up the goal completely. Why? Because the moments of crisis will come, and in that moment, the mere paper will not help you make the right decision.

On the other hand, what if instead you have an embodied vision? You visualize for 10 minutes every day in the morning how it feels, smells and looks when you cross that finish line of your first marathon. The smell of that particular city and moment. The specific people that applaud you and bring water and bananas as you kneel in tears. How it feels to be hugged by them. If you repeat this visualization exercise daily, when the moment of crisis comes (bad weather, low energy, stress at home) your body is already geared towards success. Every cell in your body remembers the visualization you did in the morning (and every morning of last week) and helps you make the right decision: *I will exercise today, even if it rains, because I am the one that will finish the marathon and get hugged soon.*

Write your goal

To start embodying your vision, write your big goal. Right now, what's your big goal? Think of something exciting and tangible to work towards. Something others can understand right away with no explanation. You can make this description so exciting that they'll feel compelled to tell others. You accomplish this by writing the goal in present tense using all the senses: hearing, smell, sight, taste, and touch. Then, start every day visualizing when you'll achieve this goal. Also, incorporate this same visualization with your team.

Consider these examples of big goals:

- Organize the world's information (Google).
- Make it easy to do business anywhere (Alibaba).
- To accelerate the world's transition to sustainable energy (Tesla).
- Remember everything (Evernote).
- Enable human exploration and settlement of Mars (SpaceX).

Sometimes, solopreneurs and athletes prefer 'dream' to 'goal', so it feels more their own ('My dream is…') as opposed to a goal. Use the word you prefer, and then follow the same formula to answer the questions below.

Create your goal

Answer the following questions to discover and clarify your goal to make it tangible.

- What is your dream or big goal?
- How does it feel to have it accomplished?
- How does it smell in that very moment?
- Who is around you, and how do they react?
- What is the best way for you to visualize this (audio, video, text)?
- When is the best moment to do this visualization (morning, evening, other)?

Now use the following questions as a checklist to refine your big goal:

- Is it something people will understand if you share it?
- Will it require you to stretch yourself out of your comfort zone?
- Is it measurable and life changing?

- Does it create momentum?
- Does it excite and stimulate you?
- Is it easy for people to tell others about it?
- Is it attractive enough for people to want to join your team?

If you said no to one of these, go back and refine it.

With your big goal clearly identified, let's create your vision for what it will be like when you get there.

Your vision in three years

If you don't have a vision, you can't reach your goals because you're not on track towards your destination. Your vision will be separate from the goal, but may include it. When writing your vision, use present tense. The idea is to zoom yourself three years forward and describe what you imagine like it's happening right now. You write from the future. Repeat this activity for your personal vision as well as your team's or your business's vision for where you want to be in three years. I have two separate guides for these two kinds of vision.

To craft your business and personal visions you use the following 18 questions. Include all five senses… smell, hear, see, touch, taste. Try to make it really vivid and alive. This is not a list like the goal-writing exercise. I challenge you to go really deep, writing five or six pages about your vision for the future.

Three-year vision brainstorm

Use the following questions as a starting point to imagine what amazing things are waiting for you three years from now:

1. How would you describe your company?
2. What does your company do?
3. How does it impact the lives of other people?
4. Who do you serve? Describe them.
5. Why is it important to do what you do?
6. How does it feel to be on your team?
7. Why are they excited to be on your team?
8. What's your uniqueness?
9. What are the main offers? Describe them.

10 How does it impact your customer's life, and their family?
11 Include pictures like a mood board. These are pictures that bring you into peak state, make you both energized and centred.
12 Who is around you?
13 How do they feel?
14 How is what you do impacting their lives?
15 Are they happy or unhappy? Why?
16 Who is around them?
17 How's the ripple effect on them?
18 How does it feel? How does it smell? What does the room look like?

For the personal vision, think about the important things to you on a personal level, not only professionally but also in your relationships and activities outside the workplace. You can also include things you stand for and your superpowers. Oh, you don't think you have superpowers? If you're not sure what your superpowers are, grab a cup of tea and answer these questions:

YOUR SUPERPOWERS

1 What do you see more clearly than others?
2 What are your three proudest accomplishments so far?
3 Which tasks come easy to you, or are effortless?
4 Which obstacles have you overcome?
5 How do you amaze others?
6 Which context suits you most?
7 When are you fearless?

Mention how you put your superpowers into service to help a specific group of people and why these parts of the vision are vital for you, your spouse, and your children. For example, I have 'I meet every challenge with courage'. You describe your best self like you're already that person. This means you state the vision as if it has happened already, and it's process-oriented, the same way it was when the start-up salespeople started saying, 'We're the global shipping software'. Basically, the personal vision describes your dream in so much detail and defines how your best self looks when it is fully unfolded. But, when you stop there, you have the same problem as with typical mission statements. You have six wonderful pages somewhere in your drawer, but no transformation occurs.

The best way to embody your vision is to start your day by reading it aloud. I do this every day, which requires a ton of discipline, but is very doable. Another strategy is to record an audio version of yourself reading your vision, and then listen to it daily. You might listen to it first thing in the morning and again before you go to bed. Repeating this vision to yourself over and over creates the muscle memory necessary so that in the moment when you make big decisions, you'll know what choices to make to keep yourself in a category of one.

Final thoughts

To be a category of one, stop doing what everyone else is doing, which makes your business as exciting as vanilla. This gives you the opportunity to define your business on your own terms. You determine who you serve in a way that no one else can come even close to matching. Then, embody your vision for who you are becoming as a CEO and for the business as a whole to evolve to that higher level for strategic goals and overall ambitions. In the coming chapters, I will tell you how to create metrics to track your progress on bringing your vision into reality with the Strategy Sprints, starting with nailing your message and brand in Chapter 2.

ACTION TOOLS

strategysprints.com/tools

CHAPTER TWO

Nail your message and your brand

> *Your mess is your message.*

Having a website for your business is an important marketing tool nowadays. If you don't have a website, you're losing the most crucial foundation of your digital marketing strategy. Your website serves as the backbone of your business. In fact, as many marketing firms have found, most consumers will research product information before they make a purchase online or in the store. This means that your website matters to your bottom line.

Showing up online with a website is good, but it needs to be designed to serve your business. Your website is your 24/7 marketing arm, so it is only right that it converts visitors to paying clients.

But the thing is...

Most websites don't convert visitors into paying customers. Leads are lost all the time because there are important messages and design elements missing from your website. Visitors become confused or disengaged and go to find your competitors' sites instead, where they easily get their questions answered and sign up. If you're experiencing this challenge, then you're in the right place.

You might be feeling like Apple's founding CEO, Steve Jobs, in 1983. That year, Jobs published a nine-page promotion in *The New York Times* called 'The Lisa Campaign'. Imagine that. Even for 1983, buying nine pages in the *NYT* was a huge expense. What do you think the nine pages were filled with? Testimonials? Beautiful images? Stories where you imagine yourself and the life you'll have when you use this product? No. That nine-page ad talked about feature, feature, and feature. It was ugly and boring, as Steve Snyder, who was working with Gates at that time, recounts in *Forbes*.[1] As a result, the campaign tanked.

So, Jobs became curious as to why his ad failed, and that quest led him to Pixar, where he learned from the best storytellers in the world. In this creative environment, he learned the five elements of a blockbuster story. Then, he came back to Apple in 1997 and made a new campaign incorporating those elements.

The new ad had no description features anymore; from nine pages to zero words on features. This Apple ad only had two words, 'Think different', accompanied by the Apple logo and an image of one easily recognized revolutionary figure, from Albert Einstein to Martin Luther King Jr, Sir Richard Branson and Steve Jobs himself. As a result, the message was clear. The target audience was clear. And Apple was on its way to becoming a major player that defined the modern tech industry.

He created this ad using these five storytelling elements:

- Define the hero and the mission: visually, this is the person in the ad, an aspirational leader that others aspire to be like as change makers.
- Pick one villain and a plan to beat them: the enemy is thinking like everyone else, and the plan is Apple. It's your ticket to be different, just like the celebrities that tout their new Apple product.
- Call to action: the words inspire you to be a revolutionary and to do so with Apple products.
- Describe success: the aspirational figures show you what your potential is when you 'think different' with Apple.
- Summarize the transformation: here, the viewer supplies the rest of the story for the bridge from where they are to where they could be with Apple products.

In this chapter, I will show you how to use the same five elements of storytelling to turn your website from a features snooze-fest into your best revenue-generating machine – in just three hours.

Fall in love with the problem, not the solution.

Step 1: Define the hero and the mission

Most websites don't have a hero, or they have defined the wrong hero. If you have 25 testimonials, then you are positioning yourself as the hero. And guess what? The people visiting your website aren't looking for heroes. They want that position for themselves. When a hero sees another hero, they say, 'Hey pal, great to see you but see you later. I'm on my own mission to save the princess – or the prince – right now.' That's why a good hero isn't your brand. Heroes are looking for a path to complete their mission, and whatever helps them on their mission they will accept immediately. They will not be price sensitive. If you help them win their day or get further on their mission, they are IN.

The hero of your offer should be who it's for, the customer or client, and they should get a sense of the outcome your offer can bring about in their lives that helps with their mission, or the problem they need to solve. When visitors first arrive at your website, they are looking to quickly decide either 'Oh, this is for me', or 'This is not for me'. So, the first picture and headline copy should speak to those concerns. Check your first picture. You will probably have to tweak it because right now I bet what it's showing for the hero and what you want to convey are not one and the same.

A website that has a clear message of the hero and mission converts people who are visitors into people who are interested to work with you. That's our goal. First, let's see why most companies do not massively convert their website traffic and will not survive the 'attention' game, in which there are so many offers that marketers are competing for attention from potential customers. **In the online world, to win this attention game, you must grab the website visitor's attention in the first few seconds, or they will click away.**

Let's do an exercise now. Take out your phone and go to your website. Look at the top section, called the 'hero section' in website design. You're about to see why. In the first seven seconds, what's your first impression? Who are you saying this is for? What are you telling them about how you help them with their mission? Do you help them achieve more freedom, more money, decreased cost, etc? If it's not clear who the hero is or how you help them with their mission to arrive at their destination, there's room for improvement. You need to create a hero.

On the other hand, if right now your hero image shows that you and your brand are the hero, you've reversed the power dynamic and are losing leads as a result. In this case, you have created the wrong hero, and you'll want to revert the hero from yourself and your brand to your customers. Don't worry, you're still in the picture, but as the guide, not the hero, as I discuss in the next section.

For now, let's define the hero. Resist the urge to lean on traditional client avatars like, 'the hero is a male, 50 years old, high income, and loves dogs'. That kind of broad view will give you both Prince Charles and Ozzy Osbourne, as we saw earlier, and it's doubtful they are both the target for the same offers. You show your perfect customer that they're your offer's hero by going much deeper. What does the hero want? Prince Charles and Ozzy Osbourne want different things. One wants to leave a royal legacy, the other a rock'n'roll legacy.

You create a much more vivid picture of your hero by getting a clear sense of their mission or what they want more than anything. Get to that deep place of knowing by asking yourself these questions:

- What are their dreams?
- What are their aspirations?
- What do they want to leave as a legacy?
- What does success look like for them?
- What does it look and feel like when they arrive at their destination?

The clarity you'll get in these answers will help you create a hero section that grabs your best customers and shows them they're in the right place to achieve their mission.

For example, think of Luke Skywalker in the original *Star Wars: A New Hope* (1977). He's the hero, and he wants to find out if what his father said is true, that he's too young to be a Jedi. And if he has what it takes to be a Jedi. That's what he wants. This mission compels him to keep looking for answers. Even many years later, the story is still compelling because there is a hero and there is something he wants.

Step 2: Pick one villain and have a plan to beat them

Continuing the *Star Wars* theme, we don't know if Luke will be successful or not, because there is a villain, Darth Vader, even though Luke has his guide, Master Yoda. So, with your hero and the mission in mind, the next thing to figure out is who is the villain or enemy to completing the mission, and who is the guide (ideally you or your offer) to help the hero be successful.

The hero has a mission, and if they could easily achieve it, they wouldn't be searching for help. The hero lands on your website looking for a guide because they have a villain or an enemy. Internal or external enemies can be obstacles to the mission, from mindset issues or limiting beliefs to lack of funding or a need for better systems. For your website to be super-clear, you'll want to choose a single villain from the possible choices and make that one the focus of your message.

For example, we say to our kids, 'You have to brush your teeth'. 'Why?' they reply. 'Because otherwise these monsters in your mouth will party the whole night.' Then, the kids can really picture what happens if they don't brush their teeth. The same thing happens in advertisements for, say, cleaning products. They don't just say, 'this product will make your room cleaner'. They paint a picture and say, 'you will get rid of these little hairy monsters in your cupboard'. This is much better than trying to list all the possible kinds of bacteria or dust mites that the cleaner kills, a strategy that would fall into the mistake of the nine-page Apple ad that bored the audience into ignoring it.

Pick one villain. The problem with most websites is they have too many villains. Due to fear of leaving something out, you will say, 'I help you do this and that and that and that'. Those lists make your reader tune out from your message and say 'Goodbye'. Another issue that can happen is there is no villain. No villain, no story. In those cases, with no enemies or obstacles, there's no need for a guide, so you are essentially writing yourself out of your own story.

Decide what external, internal, or philosophical obstacle your hero faces and choose a villain that you feel best suited to go up against. As you choose the villain, here are some things to consider:

- The philosophical struggle is the good vs bad choice. Who will win? (B2B and B2C)
- The internal struggle asks, 'Do I have what it takes?' (B2C)
- The external struggle is an actual challenge or problem the hero faces. (B2B)

While all three obstacles may be present for the reader, choose the one they're most acutely aware of and trying to overcome right now. Remember that businesses only buy the external, so if you are selling B2B, put the external struggle on the website, although keep the B2B buyer's internal struggles in mind because that is still a human transaction. If you are selling B2C, always go for internal struggles. The philosophical struggle is very general and applies to everybody in every country and type of business.

Showing that the chosen villain is your common enemy and that you know exactly how to beat them positions you as an ideal expert guide on the hero's mission.

Figure 2.1 shows an illustration of the hero's mission. You set out to describe to your website visitors how they are heroes encountering villains. Fortunately, in you they have found a guide with a plan to get them to the 'whoop! whoop!' celebration with the mission achieved.

What many people get wrong when they try to follow the hero's journey is failing to personify one villain the hero encounters on the path.

For example, let's say that you create digital calendars and complete the exercises so far:

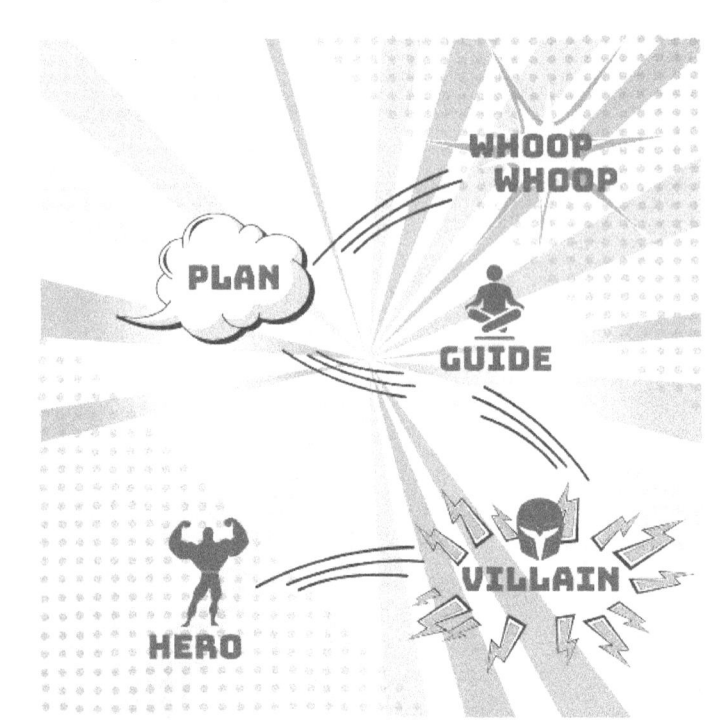

FIGURE 2.1 The hero's journey

Who's the hero? The hero is a person who is doing their best to survive the day raising four kids in Paris as a teacher.
What's their mission? They want to be a good teacher, to be a good parent.
Who is the villain? The villain is procrastination, overwhelm, not saying 'no', poor boundaries, and unrealistic expectations to complete tasks.

> *More villains are no villains.*

The above villain statement doesn't work because it's too broad, and with all those dragons to slay, it's easy to see why that teacher is going to leave and go to another website.

Picture this: they land on a competitor's page that promises to help with one villain, the one they agree on – procrastination. 'Oh,' thinks the teacher, 'procrastination is exactly what I need help with. This is amazing, like it was made just for me.' Pick only one villain, otherwise you create confusion. And if you confuse, you lose.

Personify and visualize the villain. Any villain will have all three parts: internal, external, and philosophical. For the calendar app, maybe externally, they know their calendar is a mess, and internally, they put off starting new projects. Philosophically, they want to do things when they say they will and have greater integrity. Name that. Make it visible and easy to understand. Find your internal, external, and philosophical problems – especially find a picture or a metaphor of your hero's villain. Visualize it. It needs a name, a picture so we can really interact with it, like the 'little hairy monsters' the cleaning product vanquishes.

You show more empathy with the hero the more you illustrate how compelling the villain is. We are instantly on Luke's side in the opening scene when we see his village ransacked by Stormtroopers. Then, there's the help he's offered. Luke has Master Yoda as a guide in his mission to become a Jedi. While Luke has plenty of internal struggles, he's not aware of them, but he is aware of the fight between the Empire and the Resistance, and he wants to be on the side of good, the Resistance. **The guide, Master Yoda, has a plan for just that.**

In your business, as a guide, you should offer a plan on how to start doing business with you and how to work with you to complete their mission and overcome the villain. The hero wants something, but there is a problem.

There is a villain blocking them, but then the hero meets a guide who has a plan and calls to action. This action ends in success, so that the character, the hero, will be transformed from A to B – the desired destination.

So that your website converts the heroes that land on your page to accept your plan as a guide, make it clear what the next step is. The *first plan* that you need to show is *How to start*. The *second plan* is *how you ensure the quality*, which provides risk avoidance for the hero. The *third plan* is *where can you bring me?* The promised land. Here's an example of a plan that covers all three bases:

1. Schedule a meeting with us by clicking here.
2. You get a customized report of where you are and where you can be.
3. We will send you an offer that shows exactly what your ROI is by working with us.

In order for you to create a plan of the three things mentioned above, answer these questions:

What is the plan to start with?
What is the plan for how you ensure the quality stays high?
Do you have a guarantee? What do you guarantee? How do you measure the level of quality? What happens when the quality is not high?

With the villain defined as the problem, and your custom solution, you position yourself as an expert guide to lead the hero on their mission.

Step 3: Call to action

Then comes your guidance. We know who the hero is and their mission. The villain is clearly defined with external, internal, and philosophical problems, which are personified, and you contrast yourself as the guide with a plan to help the hero achieve the mission. You present your clear plan and quality control, and then the ball is in the hero's court. Do they stay on your site and engage with your lead magnet or schedule a call, or do they leave and check out another site? That depends on your call to action (CTA).

There is a very good reason why many late-night infomercials frantically tell people to act now. You have to ACT NOW. And they are yelling at people as if they want to wake them up. They are trying to wake people up from a zombie trance. They are on their couch watching TV. And guess what? No hero ever took an action from a relaxed state. To wake up your hero, you have to create the reason, the tension, the urgency. This is a CTA from the guide.

I teach my Strategy Sprints coaches to create CTAs in two parts. There is the *warm-up* to build value in the offer and then the *solve* to make the sale. I like to demonstrate the difference in these two calls to action with a reference to *The Karate Kid* (1984). In the film, Mr Miyagi gives the Karate Kid a warm-up action, 'wax on, wax off, wax on, wax off'. In the same way that the Karate Kid warms up, you warm up your website visitors to be hot leads for your offer by giving them a call to action to perform a warm-up.

There are a few choice warm-up actions to build value for your Brand Sprint. One of these is to send people a series of emails. Another option is to send them to a Free Masterclass. You create a masterclass on how to achieve the mission the hero is going for… And you give it away for free. Another successful warm-up action is to give away an audit or a survey, something that has value. This is important. Warm-ups are only as successful as the value creation they build – because they create value that leads to a second CTA.

It's a mistake to make the call to action on your website to solve the problem. The winning strategy is to give one call to action to your warm-up. Repeat this CTA button three to four times on your site. You are the one who is calling to action. You have a plan, and now the hero must act. You provide one action: to warm up. Then, when you have built value, you make the second call to action to that warm lead to accept your offer.

Now, let me ask you… pull up your website again. What are your calls to action? Check how you are inviting the hero to act. Is it clear? Is it a warm-up? Do you repeat it at least four times? If not, make those changes and look forward to hotter website leads.

Step 4: Describe success

Show the hero what it will look, feel, sound, taste, and smell like to succeed in their mission. What's it like at the destination you'll bring them to when they work with you? That's the picture that you need to paint of how you'll lead them to make positive changes in their lives. Also, paint the opposite picture. What will failure on this mission be like? In these descriptions, you show the hero what they very much do want and don't want, positioning yourself as the guide to ensure success, without whom looms imminent failure, to be avoided at all costs.

Don't overlook the power of describing what people want to avoid. Eighty per cent of the people want to avoid something more than gaining, according to a study about loss aversion by psychologists Amos Tversky and Nobel Prize winner Daniel Kahneman.[2] They discovered that people hate much more losing $100 than they love gaining $100. So, help the heroes ditch what they are avoiding as part of your guide duties. Here are some examples:

- You will stop procrastinating.
- You will reduce your cost by 25 per cent in 14 days.
- You will never have to pick up the mail in the post office again because we will bring it to you.

What are you helping your hero to avoid? If they don't use your offer, there is a cost to it. There will be trouble for them… What is the trouble? After all, that problem is the very villain to their mission; that's why you have created a solution in the form of your offer.

Then, what does success look like if they work with your brand? That is the landscape of an accomplished mission. When you bring them there, they can clearly answer the question, 'What does success look like?' You show them:

- This is how it looks.
- This is how it feels.
- This is where it is.
- This is why you want to be here.
- These are the numbers.

Create a picture of those answers for your hero in words and images. And you need to tell, tell, tell that story on your website and anywhere else your brand has a presence.

It's up to you to create the visual and copy messages that make it clear how you help your heroes avoid failures and achieve success; when your website clearly conveys these ideals, you will gain more clients for your business.

Step 5: Summarize the hero's transformation

The last piece of the storytelling puzzle is to map your character's transformation from A at the beginning of their mission to B, arriving at success – by using your plan and overcoming the villain.

Summarize that shift in a concise and appealing manner, and you have your own transformational offer in which you bring people from point A to point B. The journey you describe shows how you help the hero succeed and avoid failure, and when you do this well, you complete your Brand Sprint.

To create your transformation summary, refer to your hero's starting point on the mission, maybe where they encounter the villain, which means they're in pain from being unsuccessful. From that pain, then create B, using your description of success. This simple statement will become your brand message, the only thing your heroes will need to know, that shows them you're the perfect guide for their mission. All the brainstorming and freewriting you've done so far will help you find the very few words that are just the right ones to nail your brand message, which should appear on your website in the hero section.

One example of a brand telling this A to B story well is Tesla. Tesla is very clear on what the transformation is. Their drivers are heroes that help the world transition from a bad old energy to a new good energy. What's the villain? Carbon. And of course, Elon Musk guides you there with his plan for you to also drive a Tesla and join his referral programme to get your friends involved in the cause, too. Now, you buy a car and become a green energy hero, and in the future, you'll probably have a smart grid, solar panel, and a battery. Those additional buying decisions will further affirm that you're a hero on a green energy mission. Do you want to become part of the Tesla story? It is not about the car. It's more about the story: the transition from an old, ignorant way of living to the new, smart one.

Final thoughts

Make the story you tell on your website simple with a Brand Sprint. Within the first seven seconds, your visitors want to see that they are the hero, not you or your brand. You position yourself as the guide with a plan to help them succeed with their mission and beat their villain. Communicate this to them in a simple A to B transformation summary. Ensure that your CTA is clear, appears multiple times, and sends your traffic to a warm-up where you then make your offer to solve the hero's issue after building value. Be clear how you ensure your offer will succeed and keep your testimonials to between three and five. In the end, you offer success and avoidance of failure. Now that you'll be converting more leads, in the next chapter I share my growth plan for your profits.

ACTION TOOLS

strategysprints.com/tools

Further reading

Campbell, J (2014) *The Hero's Journey: Joseph Campbell on his life and work*, New World Library, Novato, CA
Ogilvy, D (1985) *Ogilvy on Advertising*, Vintage, London
Strategy Sprints (2020) Double website conversion rate with this Brand Sprint (Online video) https://www.youtube.com/watch?v=MN4l-kDU7y8 (archived at https://perma.cc/5PDF-TFS4)

Notes

1 Steve Snyder (2013) 30 Years ago a deeply conflicted Steve Jobs introduced the Apple Lisa. Soon he had to reinvent himself. Here's how he did it, *Forbes*, 25 January, https://www.forbes.com/sites/forbesleadershipforum/2013/01/25/30-years-ago-a-deeply-conflicted-steve-jobs-introduced-the-apple-lisa-soon-he-had-to-reinvent-himself-heres-how-he-did-it/?sh=5b16597387ee (archived at https://perma.cc/Z4QZ-YZV6)
2 Amos Tversky and Daniel Kahneman (1992) Advances in prospect theory: Cumulative representation of uncertainty, *Journal of Risk and Uncertainty*, 5, pp 297–323

CHAPTER THREE

Your growth plan

Do you have a reliable and predictable cash flow coming in every month?

This is a question I frequently ask business owners who are interested in working with a Strategy Sprints coach. This is important because when the answer is 'no', then they're never sure where the next client is coming from and how they'll pay themselves or cover their expenses from month to month. That can lead to engaging in deals that are bad for them, and ultimately, they could possibly burn out. Because of this, our coaches work with all our clients to create reliable and predictable cash flows.

However, not having predictable revenue isn't usually a problem business owners are aware of. The notion that revenue can and should be predictable often sounds quite unfamiliar to business owners when I bring up the idea. When they think there's no alternative to scrambling to chase dollars and leads every month, they get stuck in a culture of 'the hustle'. When you're running your business like a hustler, every half-baked idea from your team gets implemented – kind of – and you say 'yes' or 'no' out of fear or anxiety. Even when you might have some wins along the way, hustling isn't a sustainable way to grow a business over time. And I bet you already know this.

What if, instead, you make all your decisions because things do or don't fit into your Growth Plan? What a novel idea. If you said 'no' to my question that opens this chapter, then like the business owners I often speak with, there is likely a hole in your business through which money and opportunity are leaking. Fortunately, there are several ways you can patch the hole or, even better, completely transform your business into one with a healthy growth model. In this chapter, I share the four Growth Levers you can pull in your business to increase revenue. Then, I lay out how you can be strategic with these levers to create your Growth Plan so you can be more profitable in a way that's predictable and leave the hustle behind.

Four growth levers

When their business isn't growing fast enough or in the ways they want it to, most business owners start trying to do different things to move the needle and increase sales. In many cases, due to fear and misunderstanding the problem, business owners throw money at solutions like marketing, SEO, sales training, etc. Those all can be important aspects of running a successful business, but they miss the point of the biggest areas of opportunity in the business – the Four Growth Levers. These are:

- Lever #1: Price and packaging.
- Lever #2: Sales time and sales rate.
- Lever #3: Systematizing.
- Lever #4: Exponential productivity.

In this chapter I teach you how to use each of the Four Growth Levers, alongside real-life examples from our Strategy Sprints clients who were struggling to grow their businesses until they decided which lever to pull and focused their energy accordingly.

Lever #1: Price and packaging

From the outside, Lara seemed to be killing it. She was a fully booked product design freelancer. She commanded $8,000 per day and was well respected in her field. But she was running out of energy. 'I'm burned out, and I have no more fuel in the tank,' she said in her first mastermind session.

She was tired of trading time for dollars. Tired of booking too much work in one month and still being afraid of not having enough work the next month. Because if she started to turn down work, clients would go find someone else they could hire immediately. Nobody waits for months nowadays. She took jobs that left her drained and miserable because she could never be certain that next month would bring more, steady work.

This is the typical feast-and-famine cycle every freelancer experiences. My advice to her was, 'Instead of working one-to-one, you need to shift to one-to-many.' And it was like a lightbulb turned on in her business. Two days after that mastermind session, her membership site was born. With that model, she could serve many more people than she did with one-to-one services, and the monthly subscriptions to her site provided consistent income. Lara won her life back.

Her income became steady, recurring, and reliable. Other mastermind participants shared how they calculate and manage the churn rates of their subscription cohorts. She now not only had a predictable sales system for the first time in her life, she also had a predictable cash flow, and that made it possible for her to make the first key hires. And that changed her game completely. She now had a business that was fun to run. She packaged her offer and started charging upfront.

In two days, you can improve your business model

To consider your price and packaging, refer to the ideal client brainstorm you did in Chapter 1. For that one client, do you have a single offer packaged at one price? If not, create one like Lara did. To create your single offer, here are some things to consider:

- What's your bestselling offer?
- Is there a cluster of services the same clients frequently need?
- What's the timeframe to deliver this offer?
- What's it worth to your client to get this help from you?
- What do you need to charge for this offer to be profitable?
- How can you build this value into the package to price it well?

Congratulations. You're well on your way to create your price and packaging. That's just Growth Lever #1, and you can already see the impact.

Lever #2: Sales time and sales rate

Tom, a copywriter, had a problem. He was working his butt off creating authority content about copywriting on YouTube every day. His offer worked quite well, as clients would pay him US $7,500 per month for his services. The problem was that people would faithfully watch his videos for eight to ten months before calling him. Despite his amazing following on YouTube, he was running out of cash. He messaged me and asked for help to reduce the amount of time leads were following him before they became clients.

I introduced him to the best growth hackers available, and he connected with a Strategy Sprints coach. They dug into his numbers and found that his sales calls were closing at quite low rates for people who hadn't been watching his videos as long. This tip led his coach to dig into Tom's sales call script. The coach gave careful feedback on every word in the script, and Tom's sales technique improved. He got better every day at closing Zoom calls. His conversion rates went from 13 per cent to 47 per cent. Also, the timeframe from people watching his videos to hiring him went from eight to ten months to three weeks.

In essence, by getting better at handling sales calls, he closed more business with brand new viewers who weren't already 100 per cent sure they wanted to hire him when they got on a call, unlike his longer-time content viewers who were ready right then to do business. Tom was smiling again. This win called for appropriate celebration, and he booked a long vacation with his wife and two kids.

Within two weeks, decrease your sales time and increase your sales rate

This might be the ideal Growth Lever for you to pull now. Often, when clients think they need more leads, what they really need is to improve their sales systems for the leads they already have. Here are some questions so you can determine where the area of improvement is in your sales process:

- Do your customers hear your offer and immediately want to buy?
- Do you know the time it takes from when someone finds you to when they hire you?
- What percentage of your sales calls become clients?
- Why aren't more of your calls converting?

When you close more of your leads and do so faster, you pull a massive Growth Lever.

Lever #3: Systematizing

Hasan was employed in a big consultancy firm making $120k a month for 80 hours per week. But his online course side hustle had started getting traction, and he decided to take it seriously. Just one problem: where would he find the time needed to grow it?

Having kids to support, he wasn't going to leave the firm before the side business was creating predictable revenue. So, he had only two hours a night to focus on developing the online course. Adding this time to his workday, he was working 90 hours per week. We worked together, and I helped him build a team to handle the online course, which skyrocketed that business. His first key hire took on tasks, some of which Hasan thought he couldn't delegate. Then, he did.

We also eliminated time-consuming activities that had a low impact on his bottom line. We focused on the highest-leverage tasks, deciding each week which bottleneck to solve next. Today, Hasan is a full-time entrepreneur, running multiple profitable online courses in just 35–40 hours per week. His income is higher, as is the time he has with friends and family, which created the freedom and happiness he was looking for.

Systematizing takes three months but scales long term with your key hires and key systems

When you feel lost in the day-to-day running of your business, the issue may be that you're doing things others can do for you. Brilliant idea, right? Then, you must conduct those hires and onboard them in a strategic way. Here are some questions to help you decide if this is your next step to grow your business:

- Which tasks give you energy, which ones take energy from you?
- How many hours are you working this week?
- Do you have team members who handle all the nitty-gritty tasks you don't enjoy?
- Could you sell your business if you wanted to?
- Can you schedule a four-week vacation without feelings of guilt?
- Which role should be your next key hire?
- What would a new CEO do if they were to take over today?

If answering these questions feels overwhelming, I have been there, and so have many of our Strategy Sprints clients. We will tackle these issues one at a time.

Lever #4: Exponential productivity

It's impossible to grow your business when you are exhausted. People will turn away from a leader who is overworked and grumpy. I know. I used to be that leader. But I was lucky to find a mentor. He shared his daily practices with me, and my life changed. They are simple, and I apply them every day. I even built templates for my team and my clients to make sure we are always high-energy and upbeat.

You cannot lead anyone if you cannot lead yourself

It might be ideal if all the Strategy Sprints business advice was about what you can do on the outside, but there are also Growth Levers within yourself. As you become the best version of yourself, this radiates beyond you to your team, the customers or clients you serve, your loved ones, and so forth. Here are some questions to find ways to become more exponentially productive:

- Do you wake up excited to build stuff?
- Do you create more than you consume?
- Do you waste time in travel or meetings?
- Are you moving the needle forward every day or just being busy?
- Are you eating well, sleeping well and exercising well?
- Do you have a strong WHY driving you?

The Growth Levers are excellent places to look for ways to increase revenue and investigate opportunities that are right under your nose. However, for predictable revenue, you don't want to always be looking over your shoulder. It's far better to create a forecast with a plan you can count on to deliver results. Your Business Growth Plan is essential in achieving success in your business. Then, you can share the documented Growth Plan with your team and lead them to implement it.

90-day growth plan

Growth is an essential part of any business. And it all boils down to the most important process you need to implement to achieve the business goals you set. This process is what we call Planning. In business, planning is essentially a business process that produces your game plan. It includes your business strategic goals, long-term vision, steps, and activities you will put in place to support and accomplish your business objectives, which may include pulling one of the Four Growth Levers, or other business-building plans that make sense for where you are now and where you want your business to be.

Your Growth Plan needs to be documented so the whole team will be onboard to support you in making the changes. When your people know about your plan, you'll work in the same direction, which results in cohesiveness. Cohesiveness creates clarity, which makes your goal achievable in less time. And when you achieve your goals in less time, then growth will be eminent in your business.

The Strategy Sprints Growth Plan maps out your next 90 days using the template available from the link at the end of this chapter. Many of our coaching clients like to complete their Growth Plans on a quarterly basis, but you can start any time. The Growth Plan details your business goals and defines your step-by-step strategies for hitting those goals. It's like a road map, a business GPS.

To create your own 90-Day Growth Plan, here are the elements to include, each of which I describe in detail below:

- Identify your main theme or vision for your business.
- Write down three goals that support your main theme. Be extremely specific.
- Clearly identify your brand positioning.
- Establish KPIs for your business so you can track progress.

You need clarity on what your 90-day forecast is so you can plan everything else, from profits to strategic investments and a marketing budget. This way, you know if you're hitting the right growth at the right speed. You cannot know if you're hitting your goal if you don't write it down and measure the progress.

Vision and main theme

When my Strategy Sprints coaches help business owners to use my 90-Day Growth Plan, the first section of the form is the Vision and Main Theme for your 90 days, as pictured in Figure 3.1.

This answers the question, 'What's your vision for the 90 days?' Refer to your notes from Chapter 1 for your short-term vision, and then input that vision here. Each time you complete a new 90-Day Growth Plan, you'll want to continue updating your short-term vision, as it will likely change as your business grows and you get closer to your long-term vision. Whatever you set as the vision, that becomes the purpose or WHY of your next 90 days.

In addition to your vision, you'll want to set a correlated theme. The theme is a single word or phrase that sets a unifying idea that everyone can

FIGURE 3.1 The vision and main theme for your 90 days

90-DAY PLAN

Vision:	Liberate 5000 owners				
	Sprint Timeline Q2 2021 APR-JUN		KPIs	Status	Owner
Goal #1:	10 Discovery Calls Per Week at CR 20% = 2 new clients per week	Josh Bullet LK Stefaan tools	10 DC per week	On Schedule	Stefaan
Goal #2:	Email Subscribers: Optimize all assets for sub collections	YT Show notes LK/LM	50 new subs/w RBS open 35% RBS click 3%	Not Completed	Michelle
Goal #3:	Appearances on: podcasts/stages	podcasts stages masterclass	# of gigs	Behind Schedule	Michelle

rally around and use to stay motivated. The vision and theme work together, as you can see in this example:

Vision: To have more happy customers.
Theme: First Impressions.

Then, you use the vision and theme to lead your team. If they bring you an idea, you can say, 'That's interesting. Does it fit the Growth Plan to get more happy customers?' You can also use the vision to determine what projects are most important to help your team spend more time on those key tasks that will move this objective forward. Also, with a theme of 'First Impressions', you can ask team members to share examples of when they have exemplified this theme or saw others create positive first impression initiatives to cultivate a culture that values this theme and carries it into all their daily work. Your vision and theme will also inform your goals.

Goal

Often, business owners set goals without first establishing a vision and theme, and this can cause chaos and confusion on a team when everyone isn't sure what to prioritize or how to measure their progress and results. In contrast, your goals will be strategic and laser sharp when they tie to creating the vision and embodying the theme. I recommend no more than three goals for any 90-Day Growth Plan.

It's important that your goals are as specific as possible, so here it's time to think about the defined milestones you want to hit within the timeframe. A sign that a goal is good is if it is measurable. An example of a growth goal can be, 'I want to be found in Google in under 1 second loading time 25 times per day.' This is good because you can measure your loading time and how many times visitors find your page. A not so good goal would be a vague, generalized objective. 'SEO optimization', for example, is not a good goal. It's not measurable, so you don't know if you are hitting your goal or not. Refer to Figure 3.1 to see an example of three goals that fit the vision and theme.

For each goal in the example, notice the corresponding columns for Key Performance Indicators (KPIs). These KPIs will help you keep track of whether you're doing the right things and making progress towards achieving the goal. Identify and put the KPIs in two categories:

1. KPIs in your control, which includes calls per week, videos published per week, etc.
2. KPIs not in your control, such as profit, revenue, and new customers.

Consider the earlier goal of your business being found on Google within 1 second; there are some things that are in your control and others that are not. Let's say that you want to rank #2 on the keywords 'business growth'. This is not something in your control, but it is your ambition, so write it down in the appropriate column, as pictured above. This is where you'll measure if you hit that goal.

Also list the things that are in your control that you will do every day and every week to make progress on this goal, such as to upload eight pictures per week with the corresponding metadata tags, upload nine videos of testimonials per week, publish 900 words of content that solves one of the top five problems of your audience, etc.

Then, every seven days you'll measure these KPIs to check your progress, which our Strategy Sprints clients do within our dashboard. Under Status, mark it properly:

- Is it completed?
- Not completed?
- On schedule?
- Behind schedule?
- Ahead of schedule?

When you achieve the given objective, take pride in changing the status to 'Complete'. Tracking your progress and recording your work as you go keeps you and your team motivated as you celebrate staying on track or even getting ahead. And when you're behind, you'll know in plenty of time to plan to catch back up.

Another thing that can happen is that when businesses get quite close to their goals, they forget to keep tracking until they go all the way to 100 per cent complete. This is how delays emerge, which can compound and slow down the organization in achieving the goals they set. We Sprinters want you to be fresh and fast so we help you close the implementation gaps all the way over your 90-Day finish line.

Another business goal in the example is 'Speed up sales cycle from six months to three months'. For this goal, create KPIs by asking, what things would you do this week to speed up your sales cycle? Great KPIs you can control might include: simplify your Value Ladder (as I explain in the Positioning section below), review your avatar and make it more precise, recheck that you're solving the three main pain points of the avatar and not just adding value, etc.

Then, there will be KPIs that are not in your control, where there's a certain level of uncertainty but progress is achievable. With this example, maybe a KPI to increase sales conversions by 20 per cent. You can measure your percentage of sales, but you can't actually make people give you their credit cards. However, this is an important number to track and shoot for a goal because it helps solve issues within the sales cycle to speed it up.

With your goals and KPIs clearly defined, it's time to review your positioning to make sure it's aligned with the 90-Day Growth Plan.

Positioning

As your goals shift to strategically focus on your short-term vision, it's necessary to check that your Positioning is appropriate to that new focus. For instance, to decrease the sales cycle from six months to three months, you want to make sure you're targeting the right leads for that quicker conversion, and you might also test different price points for the main offer, or test different offers based on this adjusted avatar. For Positioning, my Strategy Sprints coaches always double-check that the product, people, and price are right for the goals. To evaluate your positioning, refer to my

Positioning template, available at the link at the end of the chapter. Using that template, here are some questions to consider:

1. **Are we selling to the right people?** You write in the Positioning column who are the right people. In that section, you will write the avatar you created in Chapter 1. Who is the offer for? Be very precise: not just the demographics but the deep desires, pains, and dreams they have. Then, if you have validated this, check it off.
2. **Are you solving the right problem with this avatar?** Yes or No. How do you see it? If your solution solves the right problem for the avatar, your sales cycle will be quite short. Then you can tick it off your list. If not, work on your offer more to get it right.
3. **Do you really have the right price?** Ideally, you set a price that is the sweet spot for both parties concerned: you as the business find the offer profitable and your clients find the offer a no-brainer. How do you know if it's the right price? Simple. When the price is right, you sell more. You sell without hesitation. You have an irresistible offer. You're selling a lot every week, and your conversion rate is high. When that's not the case, the price may be too high, or even too low.
4. **If you have only one main product, then put YES in the next column.** If not, what's the one offer you're making to this avatar to solve their single pain point? You may have more than one offer in your business, but here, I want you to focus on just what the first thing they buy is, that first offer that turns them from a lead to a client. What is that? If you aren't sure, then answer NO. If you're still finding out what the main product is, that's something you'll want to test to figure out using your KPIs so you can learn what people are buying first and then create your positioning around that offer going forward.
5. **What's your Value Ladder?** I discuss the Value Ladder in Chapter 7, and essentially it's a series of offers that begin with one main product that's offered and purchased, followed by a series of steps up a ladder of upsells. These offers are mapped out in my Customer Relationship Management (CRM) software, so this is automated. I know at any time which relationship stage I am at with each lead and what the next action is to move them along the Value Ladder. I move them from Stage 4 to Stage 5, from Stage 5 to Stage 6, and so forth.

When your Positioning is dialled into your goals, you can create smarter campaigns that are more targeted and make amazing short-term progress on specific numbers for your Growth KPIs.

Growth KPIs

There's one more ingredient for your 90-Day Growth Plan: your Growth KPIs. These are quantifiable measurements of your results which determine how well the business performs. Some of these KPIs may be repeated from those you list for specific goals, depending on your focus on a particular vision or theme.

> *You move what you measure.*

Your Growth KPIs are important because the success of your business depends on the consistency of achieving results that bring in revenue. You need to measure your sales numbers, otherwise you may feel like you're not moving forward even when you are making progress on goals that don't directly contribute to the financials. Notice the columns in Table 3.1 that track numbers that directly impact your money.

While your business model may not include all these metrics or might include other, different ones, you'll want to track some version of the above fields to capture the correlation between your leads coming in and the revenue they generate. To choose your Growth KPIs, list your main numbers. They will be something like the following, which are represented along the top bar in Table 3.1:

- Number of qualified leads per month (#Hot Leads).
- Number of completed discovery calls per month (#DC).
- Number of customers that result from those discovery calls (#Customers).
- Total revenue.
- How happy the customers are (more about this in Chapter 9 on the Net Promoter Score or NPS).
- How much they can do in one year with you or in annual lifetime value (LTV).

Once you know where your numbers are currently for each of these metrics, start setting goals to project incremental improvement you'd like to see in

TABLE 3.1 Growth KPIs

Updated: May 5th 2021

Monthly	#Hot Leads	Conv %	#DC	Sales Conv %	#Customers	Total Revenue	NPS	LTV
Current	44	50%	22	19%	4	€62,000	76	€50,000
30 Day Target	50	50%	25	20%	5	€77,500	76	€50,000
90 Day Target	57	50%	29	21%	6	€93,000	76	€50,000
6 Months Target	73	50%	36	22%	8	€124,000	77	€50,000
12 Months Target	80	50%	40	25%	10	€155,000	78	€50,000

those numbers. *How much do you plan to improve in those 30 days, 60 days, 90 days, and long term?* Make these choices and update your numbers every seven days to monitor your progress.

Your business will grow when you follow and implement the 90-Day Growth Plan.

Final thoughts

It's time to stop hustling and instead create predictable cash flow projections. Sometimes you'll want to generate cash quickly for your business, so it might be a good time to pull a Growth Lever. You might adjust your price or packaging to bring in new sales or look at your sales process for ways to increase the sales rate or decrease the sales time. At other times, you might find more growth from creating systems or making key hires, and then there are times when you can improve yourself to grow your business. In any of these cases, it's smart to pull these levers within a 90-Day Growth Plan. This formula helps you and your team stay clear on your short-term objectives, so you track your progress and celebrate your wins on your way towards your long-term vision. You'll find out more about growing your business in the next chapter, when I break down my daily, weekly, and monthly tasks that make running a profitable business smooth and enjoyable.

ACTION TOOLS

strategysprints.com/tools

CHAPTER FOUR

Real-time decision making with the Strategy Sprints method

With freedom comes responsibility. You can never have one without the other.

CEO reality

At each stage of growing my business, I've encountered new bottlenecks and ways for me as the CEO to stop being the problem by making room for others and empowering them to do their work. This can lead to growth that you hadn't even imagined, as was the case when I first realized my marketing efforts could be smarter. I was creating and posting all the media, graphics and copy to promote my coaching programme. I noticed that other businesses cross-promoted each other's offers and webinars frequently, so I decided to build some affiliate partnerships.

Several entrepreneurs I had relationships with agreed to promote my offers, and I would promote theirs in kind. With 10 of these affiliate partners or joint venture (JV) relationships, I had solved the initial problem of marketing overwhelm. Then a friend asked me if I had a JV manager. It hadn't occurred to me that someone else could manage those relationships because they're so personal and built on trust. Then I thought about it.

Really, I was necessary during the initial outreach to create the relationship, but then someone else could manage the implementation.

Within a year of installing my JV manager, my affiliate partnerships grew from 10 to 48, but that growth didn't happen overnight. At first, the JV manager merely replaced my work. Then I realized I had time free to build more partnerships. With 48 partners, almost every week someone else is promoting my coaching programme to their audience. Today, we get around 150 new subscribers each week from our JV relationships.

In other cases, the CEO might not be the bottleneck, and growth might slow because no one owns a KPI or the associated tasks. This happened with a client of mine. They had a Facebook funnel to send leads to 15-minute calls with their sales team. People were booking the calls at a good rate, but not showing up for them. No one owned the show-up rate KPI. The client quickly realized the confirmation page and email were unclear about the value in the call and hired a top copywriter to improve the copy. This was submitted to the IT team's workload where it sat, untouched, for months because they considered these copy changes cosmetic and not functional to the coding. Meanwhile the sales team continued to have an unacceptable number of no-shows.

While on paper it seemed like all the teams were in alignment, they actually weren't. And there was bad reporting on the calls themselves, so no one was tracking the leads that returned the voice mails or answered follow-up calls to become customers. The business wasn't hitting quarterly targets; everyone was pointing the finger at everyone else while trying to make a case for themselves. Their solution was to create a new KPI for IT around implementing copy changes and streamlining the marketing processes to submit the changes in a systematic way.

This kind of problem is very common. In fact, the vast majority of business owners that start to work with a certified Strategy Sprints coach do not know:

- 'How many people are interested in buying your product today?'
- 'How many of them are 80 per cent ready to buy?'
- 'What will your sales numbers be for next week?'

Without these numbers, CEOs don't know what areas of the business most need their focus. Every month is a struggle to make reality mirror what they imagine or want. In addition to having to rely on 'fantasyland' (decisions based on hopes), their core processes are not running smoothly. They know

FIGURE 4.1 What an agile business looks like

they have too many manual activities, no modules ready, and not enough automation. In other words, they lack agility.

An agile company is not the biggest, not the strongest, not the fastest, but it is the fittest. The fittest is the one located between your customer's needs and what you offer. The fittest company has the highest fit to the customer's needs. And to continuously monitor and adapt that degree of fitness, you need an agile business that is simple, reliable, and quickly adaptable. You can see my vision of an agile business in Figure 4.1.

The flying robot fits the building blocks together and easily rearranges them. In the same manner, the Strategy Sprints method seeks to answer the question, 'How do you run an agile company?' to create your business in this vision.

To know where I was in my business so I could reshape it, I turned to my own Strategy Sprints method to change my habits. As I've previously explained, I wanted to recreate my business based on an ethos that you can take any complex issue and bring it down to its simplest parts, a minimalist approach. This reminds me of *The Minimalists: Less is Now*, a 2021 Netflix documentary. There's a scene with the host talking about the response people have when they enter his house, and it's not what you'd expect.

They don't say:

'Oh, your house is so empty.'
'Oh, I could never live like this.'
'Oh, this must have been a lot of work.'
'OMG! Who robbed you?!'

... instead, they say, 'Wow, your place is so clean.' They don't notice the lack of clutter. They focus on what's there because the items have more 'room to breathe'. It's easier to know where to focus attention as result.

I apply the same viewpoint to a business. Looking at each part on its own, I find a certain simplicity about how each part best works with the rest to create the whole, allowing for a healthy and well-functioning business. Simplicity is what's left when there's nothing else to subtract. Without the clutter of anything unessential, you're left with a business that others admire for how well it runs and how happy you, your team, and customers are.

Not only does my business thrive with these habits, but my clients do, too. From the example above, working with a Strategy Sprints certified coach, that client came to realize the funnel they were pouring money into wasn't where their happiest customers came from. Major game-changer, and suddenly the problems that kept them up at night went 'poof'. In fact, today hundreds of business owners in 114 countries use them and love my three habits, too. Experienced management consultants get certified in the Strategy Sprints method to use these habits with their clients.

The Strategy Sprints Compass

I break the habits down into daily, weekly, and monthly intervals using the Strategy Sprints Compass. This model shows a quick glance of where your business is, who's around you, and where you're going, giving you certainty to make quick decisions. Usually, we just see one part and not the whole picture, which causes us stress as we try to scan the whole environment. You need a real-time navigation to give you a sense of where you are right now, and what to do next, not months later when the P&L reports are ready. The Compass illustrates your business's departments featuring a centre and two axes, as you can see in Figure 4.2.

FIGURE 4.2   The Strategy Sprints Compass

```
        POSITIONING
    MKTG   OPS   SALES
         MINDSET
```

In this chapter, I share more about these habits that correspond to the facets of the Compass.

1. Daily habits

For 10 minutes every day, I do an Operations process from the centre of the Compass, the Time Finder. It shows me where I put my time so I can ask, *Is this the best use of my time? And what do I learn from it?*

2. Weekly habits

For one hour a week, I check in with my team on the horizontal axis for clarity on our marketing numbers, sales numbers, and client needs so we know where we are.

3. Monthly habits

For 90 minutes a month, we take a big picture of the business along the vertical axis to look at Positioning and Mindset so we know where we're going and can adjust the pace if needed.

Notice that the Strategy Sprints method eliminates all waste from traditional strategic planning: no flow charts, no long analysis phases, no interdependencies, no OKRs (objectives and key results), and no milestones. Those items limit adaptability. The three habits replace all that wasted effort with meaningful work.

The daily, weekly, and monthly habits follow a pattern of organization around the Strategy Sprints Compass, as you can see in Figure 4.3.

FIGURE 4.3 The daily, weekly and monthly habits

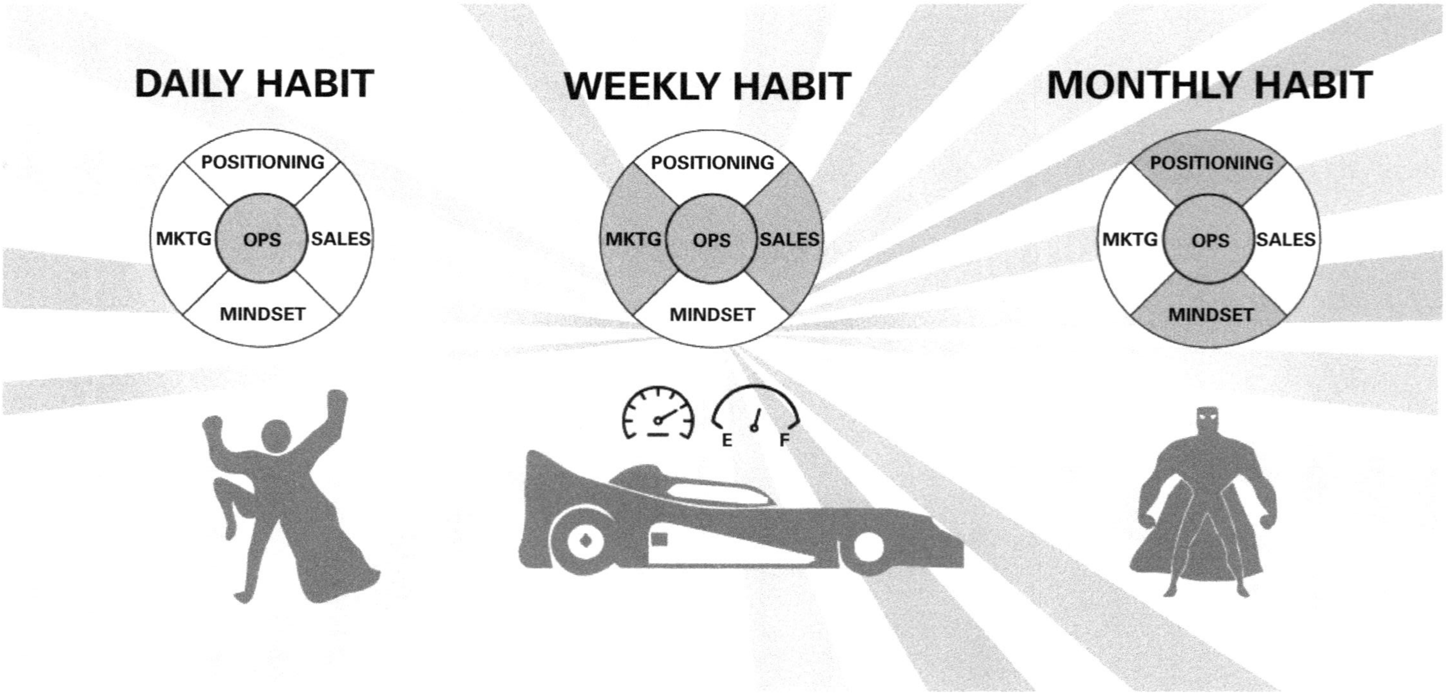

The daily habits move your needle one task at a time in your operations. Weekly habits are the vehicle that takes you where you're going through sales and marketing cooperation with operations. And the monthly habits align your positioning and mindset with your operations, which ensures the daily and weekly habits continue making sense to grow your agile business.

Do not underestimate the power of habits. They could change your life.

Daily habits

As a business owner, 24 hours is never enough to do everything. This is true especially when you're wearing too many hats – like when I did my marketing, sales and fulfilment. There wasn't enough time available to do all those things well. For a business to grow, I knew as the CEO I had to maximize my available time, so I leaned on my time management tools from Strategy Sprints. We teach that effective time management requires:

- knowing how you are – really – spending your time today;
- balancing working IN the business and ON the business;
- sensing which tasks give you energy and which ones drain your energy;
- deciding what tasks to cut, systematize, or delegate.

To answer these questions, I used the Time Finder tool our certified Strategy Sprints coaches use with business owners. With the Time Finder, in 10 minutes, we conduct four steps to grasp how you are *really* spending your time and energy right now and find ways to optimize your productivity.

Step 1

Think back to what happened in the last three days of last week. Jot down the specific tasks you did and how much time you put into them.

Step 2

For each task listed, assign each a Tier number using the categories below:

- Tier 1: admin
- Tier 2: technician is doing the work (Fulfilment)
- Tier 3: managing the work (Coordination)
- Tier 4: executive level – growth tasks, joint ventures, hiring

Step 3

Determine what energy level each task requires, between these choices:

- Gives me energy
- Takes my energy

Step 4

With the insight you gain, identify what action you'll take next for each particular task that doesn't give you energy or isn't a Tier 4:

- Cut it
- Systematize it
- Delegate it

These four steps will allow you to build a table that will look like Table 4.1.

If you get stuck here, perhaps your systems aren't well enough defined, so consider what might be missing. Often, business owners find they need things like checklists, SPOs (Standard Operating Procedures), written processes, and how-to videos. With those pieces created, proceed to delegate, automate, or find a new owner to be responsible for a task.

The Time Finder helped me see what was missing: a repeatable, reliable sales system. Up to that point, I thought, 'Okay, as soon as reliable sales come in, I can start hiring.' A catch 22 situation! Was the egg first, or the chicken? Reliable sales were never going to happen if I was spending a lot

TABLE 4.1 The Time Finder table

Task	Tier number	Energy level	Action
Task #1	Tier 2	Takes energy	Delegate it
Task #2	Tier 3	Takes energy	Systematize it
Task #3	Tier 1	Takes energy	Delegate it
Task #4	Tier 1	Gives me energy	Continue as before
Task #5	Tier 4	Gives me energy	Continue as before

of time doing client work. With this insight, I fired myself from fulfilment tasks. But I didn't cut them. I created a system around them in an online certification course and delegated the tasks to people certified in my method. In this way, I multiplied myself and wasn't the bottleneck anymore. And I did it again when we adopted the JV model.

I focused my daily tasks on Tier 4 activities like quality control, supervision, sales, and joint ventures, so I went from having a job to running a business. The business model now was viable and healthy because I had enough time – eight hours per day – to work ON the business and not in the business. This has changed everything and made me feel like the flying robot in Figure 4.4.

Ready to supercharge your battery and soar with your agile business? Here are two more daily habits to end your day strong:

1 Write the flow of tomorrow: What is the hard landscape (calendar)? What are the top three things this week? When will you do the tasks that give you energy? When will you do the tasks that take your energy away?
2 At the end of the day, take three minutes to reflect: Which of today's activities could be done by somebody else even better? If I lived more intentionally and freely I would…

FIGURE 4.4 A full battery and a soaring agile business

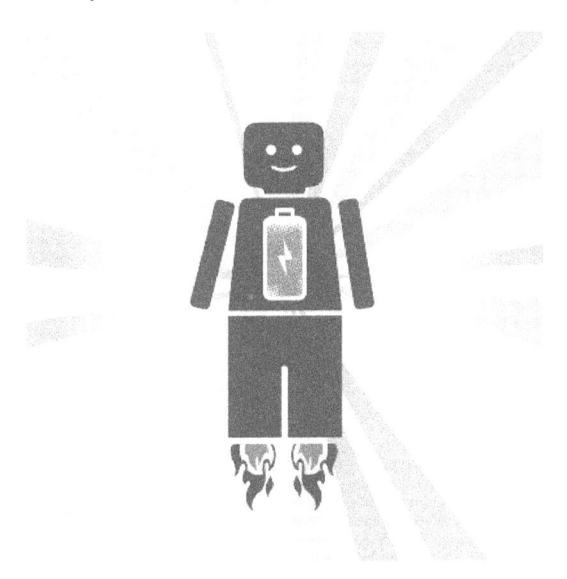

Weekly habits

Before we started the weekly habit, I had no idea what my projected sales were from week to week, and I went after every marketing tip that sounded hot, from Clubhouse to LinkedIn. I didn't know which platforms were bringing in clients or what was important to track. Impressions? Clicks? And for the things I really wanted to know – *are people on this platform buying from me?* – how on earth could I tell? With all these unknowns and thinking everything was important, our meetings felt very corporate and would go on for hours trying to hash out the problems. Things had to change.

So, we started a weekly habit to schedule a one-hour meeting to get reports on marketing numbers, sales numbers, and operations numbers, reflecting the horizontal axis of the Strategy Sprints Compass. I suggest looking at these numbers weekly because they change so much from day to day. This habit transformed long, painfully boring meetings into shorter meetings that feel like friends playing basketball. Instead of allowing people to bring problems to the meeting, like not booking enough sales calls, I switched to allowing solutions only, based on the numbers. In other words, only prototypes or theories and hypotheses, such as, 'Perhaps x is why we're not booking enough sales calls, and I propose trying y to increase them.'

> *No prototype, no meeting.*

Below, for each weekly report, I list the kinds of information our certified Strategy Sprints coaches review with clients:

- Marketing numbers
    - How many people were interested in us this week?
    - How many people did we get on our calendar this week?
    - How many people are warm leads and hot leads? (We need to make them hot.)
- Operational numbers
    - How happy are the clients this week?
    - What do we need to solve for them?
    - Do we have everything, or do we need to build something for them?

- Sales numbers
  - How many people did marketing get on our calendar this week?
  - How many of them did we close?
  - What's the conversion rate?
  - What do we learn from the gap?

Making this horizontal axis a weekly focus gave me the clarity I needed to understand *where* my business was to create balance and sustain it even in times like the pandemic when market conditions suddenly changed, and I had to change my business accordingly. Now with our Strategy Sprints Dashboard our meetings are just a few minutes long. We can track our numbers at a glance and celebrate when we hit them, and when one goal is achieved, we set another one and go after it together. Join us in the weekly habit and get your FREE Dashboard from the Action Tools link at the end of this chapter.

Monthly habits

Implementing the weekly habit was liberating, but we still didn't have the full picture of the business. For the CEO view, I needed a specific time and way to create the vision for our growth. While that was impossible before, with the Strategy Sprints Dashboard, it became possible. I had predictable revenue and was sleeping better at night – no more putting out daily fires – so I was in a suitable state of leadership to reflect on our *strategy*.

The monthly habit, or vertical axis of the Strategy Sprints Compass, introduces strategy for positioning and mindset. I see the breakdown of habits like swimming. When you swim long distances, your head is down in your daily habits. Then, you come up for air at regular intervals with weekly habits. But you don't want to run your business just staying afloat. When you're swimming, from time to time you have to check:

- 'Am I swimming in the right direction?'
- 'Do I like where I am now?'
- 'What can I learn from where I've been?'

You wouldn't want to tread water for days, so we do 90-minute monthly meetings to briefly pull your head out of the water, check where you are, where you have headed, and who else is there. Then, head down again, and keep moving forward.

This third habit that Strategy Sprints certified coaches implement with business owners is the monthly meeting to enable your focus, freedom and flow to emerge. Positioning is something I was never able to focus on when I was always swimming in my business and not coming up for air, and mindset seemed like a luxury I lacked time to tackle. These are important elements of being that CEO who sets the GPS coordinates for the business and leads in that direction.

For positioning, we measure this by tracking our feedback score obsessively. Feedback is the breakfast of champions, as I discuss more in Chapter 9. It can feel like you are making yourself vulnerable to ask the people you serve how you're doing, but this openness makes you stronger. The customers feel that you truly care, which builds their trust. This is the difference between being a brand and a partner. We want our customers to feel cared about and heard, to succeed. We also see from these numbers that if they are happy, we really are delivering on our promises, which makes us even more confident with marketing and sales. Good feedback scores create a positive feedback loop that can impact the mindset as well. I often find there's a correlation with poor feedback scores and lower mindset scores, too, and it is important to interrupt those negative feedback loops as they occur so they don't continue.

Here are the kinds of topics we evaluate in the monthly meetings, using our feedback scores:

- Are we selling to the right people?
- Are we selling to the right people *at the right price*?
- Are we differentiated enough?
- Are we in the right marketing channels to reach our customers?
- Are we absolutely not comparable to anybody?

Answering these questions will help you change direction when necessary, and will help you differentiate your business and get back on track.

In addition to positioning, we work with business owners on their mindset. Business champions need two things: skills and confidence. You need both because high skills yet low confidence stops you from taking action. You already have the skills but you also need the confidence that you're the right person and can deliver the right value you promised so you can keep swimming. That's the mindset you need to achieve.

When feedback scores are high and mindset is too, the meetings end early, which makes us all happy. At other times, maybe feedback scores are high, but along with that can come 'imposter syndrome', a fear that you're afraid the customers might find you out for not being amazing, but instead a flawed human doing your best. In this case, a low mindset score would contrast a good feedback score. For lower or average feedback scores, there might be a correlation with mindset scoring lower. It makes sense that confidence to sell and deliver will fall when the customers aren't happy. Also, if there's a high mindset score and a low feedback score, as CEO, you might come to terms that what you believe is true and what your customers believe aren't matching up – so you can address it.

We ask one mindset question and ask the team to rate themselves on a score of 0–100: 'How confident are we that we're the best solution to our client's problem?' If anyone responds 99 or less, we investigate why they're not 100 per cent confident and how to turn that into 100. We look at where the uncertainty is coming from – skills, solution, product, offer, competition, etc – until we find the area of opportunity and address it. It's not enough to be the best. You must also believe it because of Confidence Transfer, which is the gap between your belief and the next person's confidence in your offer. The gap of belief is usually 30 per cent, so if you have 100 per cent belief, the customer may have 70 per cent. This slope goes downhill fast, because if your belief is 70 per cent, this puts your customer at 40 per cent. The gap holds true even when you say all the same scripts as you do when you're at 100 per cent but on a day with 70 per cent belief; your customers won't believe you the way they will when you say all the same things from a place of deep conviction.

I find that doing this monthly habit is great to make sure I believe everything I say, so my clients will, too.

Final thoughts

As you see with the daily, weekly, and monthly habits, your business is a system made up of small, simple pieces you can change very quickly. The daily habit shows you how important every hour is and how this affects the growth of your business. Then, the weekly and monthly habits reveal that sometimes you need time to pass to best review certain parts of your business, and reviewing those elements doesn't have to waste time when you use the Strategy Sprints.

With these three habits, I went from struggling, hustling, and fighting every month to a calm and organized way of running a business that is agile and resilient. I now have time for my family, for my kids, friends, reading books, exercising, etc. Use these habits to make quick decisions and with clearer direction by managing your time strategically. In the next chapter, I return to the idea of the daily flow in even more detail.

ACTION TOOLS

strategysprints.com/tools

CHAPTER FIVE

Daily flow

> *If you don't run the business, the business will run you.*

'Don't tell the clients to expect a call back, even if they are unhappy,' the regional manager snapped at a call centre representative. 'There's no way I can call them until 3 pm tomorrow because I am in stacked meetings.' The angry client called back twice before the regional manager returned the calls, and by then the client only wanted to cancel their membership immediately.

A COO client shared this story with me, which illustrates their team's struggles to decide what was most important and get those things done. And if the regional manager wanted to delegate that call, there wasn't anyone else trained to take on that task. The COO was in the same boat. He had too many projects, and one of his team members had noticed: 'It seems like in our sprints, we never finish what we started. We just start on the next goal.' That's how it was going, and then they would set another goal and continue rushing around to put out fires.

No matter how much it seemed like everyone was doing, revenue remained stagnant. Even as they added new members, they lost the ones they had, so growth was at a standstill, and it seemed like there was nothing more anyone could do. Everyone was stressed out, from the employees facing the clients to the C-suite, and something had to change. The business was running them, instead of the other way around.

'If you had to name a single problem here, what would you say you need more of?' I asked him.

'Time!' he said.

Did you know that many business owners are time-poor? We all have 24 hours in each day and prioritizing how you spend yours is perhaps the most important business decision you make every day. Yet, most business owners don't think strategically and can end a whole workday without making significant progress on any particular goals. Time is often your most valuable resource, and most entrepreneurs need all the help they can get to maximize it to get optimal results and achieve freedom.

For business, productivity growth is important because providing more services to clients translates to higher profits and dictates your business growth speed. As productivity increases, a business can turn existing resources into revenue and keep profits in order to grow and scale the business, which leads to your competitive advantage against your competitors, who will struggle to keep up with your output. When you have optimal productivity, you can get things done in less time. And this gives you more resources to utilize to help achieve the freedom that motivates most entrepreneurs to start a business in the first place. Of course, there are different forms and definitions of freedom from person to person. I imagine freedom like I'm floating above it all, as you can see in Figure 5.1.

What is your idea of freedom? Whatever it is, your business is your medium to make it happen.

> *Productivity is about creating freedom.*

As entrepreneurs, we all want to reach freedom as soon as possible. This can be achieved by increasing productivity, to get more done in less time instead of spending more time on tasks. For me, this is the most important achievement as a business owner. Your time freedom starts with the daily habits in Chapter 4, and then in this chapter I build onto those habits and go deeper into my top three systems to maximize your productivity:

1 **The Project List.** This is a list of all your projects around your life and business, including the end date and their definition of 'done'.

FIGURE 5.1 Productivity growth leads to more freedom

2 **The Daily Flow.** This is a set of actions you need to do daily to support the completion of your projects.
3 **The Protection Systems.** This is a support system you put in place to protect your focus and productivity. The goal is to complete your important priorities first before anything else.

I maximize every day with the above three systems that help me run my successful global business and regain my time freedom. You'll find that these three systems will help you run much of your day-to-day business activities on autopilot so you have more time and freedom to do the things that make you happy and that only you can do.

The project list

I first heard about creating a Project List from David Allen,[1] creator of the 'Getting Things Done' (GTD) method, and I've interviewed him several times on my podcast. His concept of the Project List helps you stop complicating your life with different flows, processes and timelines. You just make a list of your main projects and then break them down. Take out a piece of paper or open a notes app and start listing the projects on your mind that you would like to accomplish. You may find that there are a lot of them, and on a daily basis, this makes it tough to prioritize what needs to be done right away. Your projects may all be worthy of completion and be great ideas, but to make significant progress on them, you need to keep them organized with their own game plans, and the Project List will help you accomplish this.

In my case, at any one time, I'm thinking about around 10–15 projects. For example, below is my current Project List:

- Book draft
- CEO out of sales
- JV Google
- JV law firm
- Federico swim practice
- Alessandro music practice
- NPS from 64 to 84
- Ted Talk
- Sales team
- Hiring editor
- Hiring Sprint Coaches

Right now that Project List adds up to 11 projects. That's too many major projects to balance or make progress on. What's your Project List like? Make a list of your top agenda items, both personal and professional. I bet that will feel overwhelming, and this is the case for many of our Strategy Sprints clients. We need to narrow your focus so you can start completing projects.

Within your list of all the projects on your mind, isolate each one and create a game plan for it. This game plan will begin with an end date and a definition of 'done'. As you can see, for the top item on my list, 'Book Draft', below I formulate a game plan to finish writing it.

#1. I will write and finish a book draft by Christmas.

Notice that I did not write the details of how I will finish the task, but I have exactly formulated its end date and a definition of 'done', which I can share with my team. Business coach Jeff Sutherland writes in *Scrum* (2014) that a definition of done (DoD) is a 'shared understanding of expectations' that the project in question will meet a certain criterion to be considered 'complete'. This means that the parties involved – here, my team and me – agree on just one definition or criterion for this project to be considered complete.

Upon sharing this DoD with my team, they had some questions about what it would really mean to finish the book draft. Does that mean it's all ready to publish? Would that mean all the images are created? Will we be working right up to Christmas Day? With these thoughts in mind, we refined the project to:

The book draft will be ready by 21 December. It should be 12 chapters in total. All 12 chapters need to be edited, produced, and ready to be published.

This clarified DoD is even more clear and measurable, and that's the point. Your Project List isn't a one-way street where you decide the criteria and deadline and then legislate it. Instead, the DoD needs to be mutually agreed upon so your organization can work together as a team towards the goal and not stop until you achieve it.

Let's try this again with the second item on my Project List:

#2. CEO out of sales and implement a sales team that is fully trained and performing by Q3.

As you see in Chapter 4, my previous project was to get me as the CEO out of fulfilment, and that outcome materialized last January. And to take my business a notch higher, I set a new goal to further level up and get out of the sales role. When will I know it is done? It is very clear that this project will be complete when I do less or zero sales per week, and the team does it exclusively. In this game plan, I am not further explaining how the sales training will happen or what implementation will look like because those are pieces of the puzzle best supplied by the people who will take on those tasks. This is another way that I avoid a very top-down leadership role that ignores the creative power and expertise of the very people I hired for those reasons.

Going further down my Project List, you'll see in #5 and #6 that my kids are also part of it. You might be thinking, *Simon, this is a personal project and is not in any way related to the business. Why did you include it in your Project List?* This is something I learnt from David Allen. He told me, 'You don't have to separate your business and your life. It's just one thing. It is really powerful when you're un-dividedly centred into one thing.' How profound. Think about it. Complexity is the enemy of clarity. Even complexity in your identity or the roles you have in different areas of your life can distract you if those roles are not all unified. Considering all your projects, both personal and professional, in context of each other is important to achieve the clarity and focus you need for maximized productivity.

It is important to check each project off the list after it is done and celebrated. Don't forget to celebrate the significant milestones in your business.

On my Project List, we are remarkably close to completing the #7 focus on the feedback score, which is the indicator that shows how happy our clients are with us. Currently, our feedback score is 64. Our DoD is to move the score to 84 by the end of our next 90-day Sprint. As you can see, the goal is quite clear and specific for what we're measuring and when we want to achieve it. Then, once this is achieved, we can tick this off our list and applaud everyone that helped to complete the project. Sometimes it's enough to thank or acknowledge key players in a team meeting by arranging a special dinner or refreshments; other times you might want to send them a gift or even award a cash bonus, depending on the circumstances and what's appropriate in your business. In any case, we never want to complete a project and then go to the next one with no pause for applause because that would be a joyless work environment – no fun for you or the team.

In my Project List, I keep it simple and share when the project starts and when it ends – the project DoD. Notice that:

- There is only one next action.
- There is no milestone.
- There is no interdependency analysis.
- There is no risk analysis.
- There is no budget.

But the truth is, there is a budget in place. I just didn't place it there as it would be a distraction, which is the same for the milestones, risk analysis, etc. My team uses these simple project DoD headlines that stick to the completion criteria and due date in our shared dashboard housed by Asana. Every day, I review the Project List in just five minutes to know what's most important to accomplish that day. The outcome of my reviews influences my next strategy, the Daily Flow.

The daily flow

How much happier and more productive would you be if you had a predictable routine that allowed you to always complete your most important tasks? Many entrepreneurs instead put out one fire after another and end the workday exhausted and no closer to their goals. That's because they let external events dictate their schedule instead of orchestrating it themselves. Observe the two robots in Figure 5.2 and notice the depleted energy of the one on the left, compared to the fully charged one on the right.

FIGURE 5.2 How our Daily Flow can influence our energy levels

The difference between having the energy of the left versus the right robot comes down to one thing: having a Daily Flow. Consider using the template shown in Figure 5.3 and follow along as I explain how it works.

I construct my Daily Flow based on weekly goals that I then break down into daily chunks to make the work measurable and manageable. And I schedule everything, including my fitness routine, so nothing personal or professional falls through the cracks if there's a tight deadline.

My Daily Flow is planned right down to 15-minute intervals in some cases. Along with each day's flow, I also include a list of my top priorities for the week. These are derived from my Project List. I encourage you to choose no more than three projects from your list on which to focus on a weekly or daily basis. That's because focusing on too many projects is unreasonable and can lead to errors or slow down your progress on any single project.

With your top three projects selected, then you want to create action items to make progress on those DoDs. Ask yourself: *What activities will I do to make the top three priorities happen?* Then, make room on your Daily Flow for those activities. A word of warning – don't mistake this advice for another to-do list. As *Indistractable* (2019) author Nir Eyal notes to me in his Strategy Sprints podcast interview: 'Forget the to-do list. It is much more important how much you put into the work because a to-do is just dreaming that something happens. But you must put in the work, and the work is

FIGURE 5.3 Daily Flow

strategy sprints

DAILY FLOW

What are the three most important tasks of this week?

List out your schedule for the day: known events and commitments, plus when you will work on each task above.

TIME   ACTIVITY/TASK

Which of today's activities could be done by somebody else even better?

If I lived more intentionally and freely I would:

NOTES, ETC

Strategysprints.com

on your calendar.'[2] So, you decide what activities you must do, and then you set aside the time to do them. Without that second step, there's no predictable relationship between your daily activities and moving the needle on your top projects.

You might notice that my day has a flow that starts with working out and spending time with my family, and then after I do some work, I lift weights and have lunch. Then, it's back to work, followed by family time. This is a way that I create freedom in my business. It is a good flow for me because there is enough space for happiness, which is my family. There is enough exercise with the two workouts. There is enough movement for the business to go forward on the top three priorities. For me, that is a balanced day and a Sprinter's day.

Then, at the end of the day, I put on my CEO hat. It's time to think beyond completing activities and consider how I can be a better leader and happier business owner. To discover these answers. I review two reflective questions:

1 *Which of today's activities could be done even better by somebody else?* It's important to regularly analyse what actually happened in your day that followed or deviated from the flow. Identify the tasks that could perhaps be delegated to someone who can do the activity as well as or even better than yourself. Also notice what activities could be systematized.
2 *If I lived more freely and intentionally, what would I do?* Answering this is like describing your ideal Daily Flow. You imagine doing the things you want to do without any limitations or boundaries.

Here's an example of my reflection on the second question:

> I could manage and grow my pipeline from the beach because the business is systematized. I could scale my business anywhere. Now, I can choose the temperature and the humidity of the country I am in. I am free now. I'm not stuck in one place anymore.

With this idea in mind, it was clear that in reviewing the first question, I needed to delegate and systematize marketing and admin tasks. That idea then goes on the Project List and becomes a team effort. If all this sounds a bit idealized, you'll see how I stick to my Daily Flow even when unexpected things happen with my Protection Systems.

The protection systems

As a business owner, you must protect your time, and that's what this chapter covers. But the thing is, sometimes not everything goes as planned. There are some slight hiccups or delays. Sometimes life happens and brings you out of your plan. These are random things that pop in, like a delivery delay or someone giving a 30-day notice. For things like these, I'll put those issues in a place where I can attend to them later and not in the moment. I handle things accordingly, and it's my decision to do so – at the right time. It might be this evening. It might be tomorrow morning.

The bottom line is, I'll find a place and time to handle it. I will also tell the people involved when I am going to deal with it, so they're not left hanging, and yet the surprise will not destroy the flow of my day. This is about protecting your sanity and your zone of genius. Your zone of genius is best activated when you channel it into your daily activities that feed your top three priorities.

Often, the challenges to your zone of genius aren't even so dire. For example, you open your browser because you are researching something. You are Googling something but then you go AHA! Minutes tick by, and you go from one page to another, which brings you to what I term 'infinity pools'. Infinity pools are things that get you in the rabbit hole of spending more time than you allotted on a task, leaving your focus on the table. Currently, my infinity pool is Instagram. For example, I was researching somebody's current role and position because they were a guest on my podcast. Checking that account's feed led me to other unrelated topics. Something about yoga interested me. Then, I viewed something else related to CrossFit and endurance. *Then I was lost.* I lost 10, 15, 20 minutes of the day and did not move the needle on my top three priorities.

This is why I have Protection Systems to limit or entirely avoid deviating from my zone of genius when issues arise, or I discover a rabbit hole. All those distractions bounce off my Protection Systems as depicted in Figure 5.4.

The zone of genius shields in my protection system are Momentum, Asana and Slack, and Gmail Blocker. These exact tools and software may not be what you need but notice how they solve problems for me and how I use them so you can identify where you can better protect your zone of genius with systems.

Momentum is a Google Chrome extension that replaces a new tab page with a personal dashboard featuring to-do, weather, and inspiration. Every

FIGURE 5.4   Zone of genius protecting shield

time I open the browser, I see a nice picture that includes a link to my top three priorities. This helps me not to get distracted with browsing and serves as a reminder that I only need to search for things that move the needle on the three priorities.

In this case, the priorities are being pulled from **Asana**, which, as I mentioned, is where my team's dashboard is housed. There, we communicate on project updates and house our spreadsheets and assets, so everything is in one central place. We also use **Slack** as a communication channel for our team and our clients to send messages and have conversations, which I can monitor if I choose, but which can also happen without my presence, freeing up my time for the top priorities.

Another protection system I rely on is the **Gmail Blocker.** As a Gmail user, I can install this plug-in that tells it when to deliver my emails. I set it so that I never get an email before noon. I do this because before 12 o'clock I don't access my inbox. This is on purpose, because as you have seen in the flow of my day, I don't want to be disturbed while I'm doing activities related to my top three priorities. Then, by the middle of the day, I'm done with those activities and can turn my attention to what's happening in my emails. In fact, I am usually done before 10:30 am.

I also exercise strict controls on what I allow into my inbox at all to keep it organized. You may be amused that I only have three folders in my inbox: 1)

ACTION, 2) Action support, and 3) Templates. Anything that doesn't fit these categories gets deleted or delegated. Also, my iPad, iPhone, and MacBook notifications are always 'off'. This gives me control of my time, because I decide when I give attention to which thing.

With these Protection Systems in place, I eliminate a lot of time-sucking distractions and stay in my Daily Flow, so I keep making progress on my top priorities and have the freedom to do what makes me happy.

Final thoughts

Avoid being time-poor and increase your productivity as well as that of your team with these daily systems. It is especially important to identify the top 10–15 projects you want to complete. For each, set the definition of 'done' and a clear deadline. Decide which three of these projects will be priorities in any given week, and then schedule activities that support those outcomes. And don't forget to also *do the next actions*. Focus only on the next action. No milestones. No interdependence analysis. No risk analysis. Just the next action. Then, try to do the most important thing in the morning and protect your focus hours. Protect your Daily Flow with Protection Systems to organize and systematize your work and communications and avoid infinity pools. Shut off the notifications and decide with intention when you are going to do emails. At the bottom line, productivity is about creating while maximizing your resources to give you optimal results – results that will get you closer to your freedom. In the next chapter, I go deeper into winning weekly systems and how to delegate like a boss.

ACTION TOOLS

strategysprints.com/tools

Notes

1 Allen, D (2015) *Getting Things Done: The art of stress-free productivity*, Piatkus, London
2 Strategy Sprints (2020) 'How to be Indistractable with Nir Eyal', https://www.strategysprints.com/blog/how-to-be-indistractable-2 (archived at https://perma.cc/MAS7-33PP)

CHAPTER SIX

Find traction instead of distraction in your ideal week

> *If you don't have time, you don't have priorities.*

Have you ever tried to play football without proper studs? It would be a disaster of slipping and sliding on the turf. You'd have more misses, slips and falls. Your precision would suffer. As a child, you might play football casually without studs, but once you're on a team and playing for real, you need shoes with the proper bottom that give you a competitive advantage. Those studs provide traction, which prevents many slips and gives your footwork more laser focus.

Well, you don't want to run your business with the precision of a child playing a casual game, do you? Lacking full control of your movements and whipping out. No, I bet you're a business owner who wants to make deals and run plays like a skilled athlete with proper gear. And to do that, you need proper traction in your business, which allows you to create space and boundaries to really stay on the playing field of your game.

The choice is between living your life on purpose (with traction) or staying in reaction mode (without traction). These days, it's rare for busy entrepreneurs to plan their week and think things through. Instead, they tend to go with the flow, spending their time agreeing to their business demands instead of getting their priorities straight beforehand. Because of this, when most business owners complain that they don't have time, especially if they're wearing too many hats inside their business, the truth is that they're not making time for the important things.

This is a tough pill to swallow, but if something matters to us significantly, we will make time for it. So, shifting your mindset from having no time to having enough time is done by simply changing how you approach and clarify your priorities. And if you want to grow your business, you'll do so more easily with clarity on what are your high-value activities that significantly impact your business. Those give you the traction of football studs. If you prioritize these activities, you can do better, more meaningful work that will bring your business to the next level.

Making these choices starts with being proactive and mapping out your 'Ideal Week' for your business. An Ideal Week is a powerful tool that helps you design your week according to your needs and where you want your business to be. This is important because if you don't do it, loads of meetings and to-dos will pile into your calendar, and you will be scrambling without a plan.

I know what you might be thinking. I'm not going to tell you about creating the unrealistic Ideal Week where you are spending time on an island and just surfing the whole day. This is a more practical, ordinary 'Ideal Week' that gives you a framework for how you operate, your patterns, and your strengths and weaknesses. The Ideal Week is like a glue that connects your best life and business with your daily specific actions that support your higher goals.

So, for example, I have a simple rule that I always follow when it comes to protecting my Ideal Week's boundaries: in the morning, I do my top three tasks because I have optimal energy in the morning. Plus, I have fewer distractions since most people are not working yet. This is my time to create material for myself and my business, while maintaining my pace and momentum. As a result, I get more things done in less time while growing my business faster.

In the afternoons, I have meetings, joint ventures and discussions about deals, business growth, collaborations, or I coach our coaches. I created this Ideal Work Week because I know when to say YES and when to say NO. It's as simple as choosing when you'll do the activities you choose to do, and then refusing the rest.

When you decide what your ordinary Ideal Week looks like and have this blueprint, make it visual as an addition to a Google calendar or just put it on the wall. You'll make many micro-decisions every day that will gradually evolve your week to become that Ideal Week. With this strategy, if somebody asks for a meeting, you can accept an appointment whenever you have designated time for that appointment type. For example, I am available to meet with vendors on Friday mornings; vendors have to adjust their calendars to mine. This forms part of your Ideal Week.

Life isn't always perfect, but you could have an Ideal Week every week if you chose to do so. As I explain in Chapter 5, you can either design a business where you are in control, or your business controls you, and we considered this within the ideal day. In this chapter, I build on that concept to explore how all those ideal days stack together into creating an Ideal Week for maximum business traction in four steps:

Step 1: Map your Ideal Week to take control of your time.
Step 2: Create traction in your business to know what activities to prioritize.
Step 3: Add time blockers to your calendar so there's time to do what's more important.
Step 4: Respect your personal energy patterns to set reasonable goals and avoid burnout.

Your business can stop happening to you and become a tool you control to create the life, income, and impact you choose. Let's do it.

Step 1: Map your ideal week

We begin with a GPS view of all five business days of the Ideal Week. Think of each day like a house on a block of five houses. As of yet, there are no details about how many parking spaces there are or if they all have a chimney. Those are details you are going to start filling in, metaphorically, for each day. Use the Ideal Week template available on our website, which you can find a link for at the end of this chapter. Or pull out some paper and collect your ideas, beginning with a list of five daily intentions set for Monday through Friday.

Begin by setting an intention for every day. By deciding for each day what the most important focus will be, you set the stage to then only choose activities on that day that will contribute to this intention. Let's say you decide that Mondays are a 'Sales Day', if you're still taking sales calls. Then, it will be simple to choose activities that help you sell more and fill that day with more of that work. You might get more specific and decide, 'My goal is setting sales calls for the sales team to close.' Here, you are also delegating what part of sales you are involved with and what is for your team. You can even go a step further to decide, 'On Mondays, I will reach out to 200 people so that 10 of them schedule a call with the sales team.'

Or if you are a 'closer', you might set the intention for 'Closing Deals'. Then, you wake up in the morning with 10 calls in your calendar, and you challenge yourself to close at least five of them. Then it is a 'Closing Day'. Choosing one day to focus on sales keeps the rest of your week clear of sales calls or activities, which can often dominate a business owner's week and prevent other important projects from moving forward.

Another day might be the 'Team Day' when you are available for teammates to have one-on-one meetings with you – time when they know they are invited to put themselves on your calendar if they need your help. This helps you never feel like your people are bothering you and gives them a structure so they're not constantly asking for your time every day. You also empower your team to take initiative and solve more things on their own, which is good leadership.

You might also have a 'Marketing Day' to record videos for your clients or weigh in on copywriting projects and create other kinds of content. This kind of work, which has an uncertain outcome, tends to get pushed to the backburner if it's not in the calendar. But companies that consistently create and share content elevate their credibility and expertise, allowing them to grow faster and sell more. I will share much more on the topic of marketing later in this book.

As you create new 90-Day Sprints, your intentions for the Ideal Week may shift with new goals and priorities, so let this be a flexible process that changes with your needs. Depending on your business model, other days you might choose to focus on could be:

- Strategic Partnerships Day
- Employee Hiring and Onboarding Day
- Fulfilment Day
- Public Relations Day

For any day's intention that you set, try to make it as specific and measurable as you can. This will help you choose the right number of activities to make progress towards those outcomes. Basically, set daily intentions that will serve you and your business – no hard rules for this. Let your creativity do its magic.

Step 2: Create traction in your business

After you've set intentions for each day, think about what the elements that make up your week are. These elements are activities or issues that regularly come up either daily or weekly, and when you have this awareness, you can choose when you will address them within the Ideal Week. For now, create a list of these elements that you'll plot on the calendar in Step 3. This is how you create traction and take control of your time, rather than letting these elements control your priorities. Just like how studs give a football player traction against their momentum and the grass, planning when you address these elements stops you from feeling like you're always dusting yourself off and getting nowhere.

For example, if reviewing your sales team's material before they present to a client is a regular element of your week, decide what day this activity fits into and schedule time to do the reviews then. This will be life changing. Your team will know the deadline and when to expect your feedback, and you know when you're going to do that work.

Another element that I find applies to most of our Strategy Sprints clients is fulfilment. This category of activity involves building the product. So usually, one leader's activity is coding, building, building, coding. And another person in the company does the selling in the first years. Your primary fulfilment might be building the product, coaching, consulting and teaching, etc. In the next step, you'll see in the template that this element is red because this is the colour we want to get off your plate and delegated as soon as possible. And these activities can dominate all five days if you don't keep these roles in check.

There's also the element of growth, which is a CEO topic. Sales are also part of the growth, but growth is more than that, as I discuss in Chapter 3. Growth is the business of business, working 'on' the business. These tasks are when you work on the form, fit and function of your sales process, marketing process and fulfilment process. This includes your vision, positioning, joint ventures, collaborations, franchise system, affiliate system, blue ocean strategy, etc.

There are some other elements that you'll want to plan for within the Ideal Week. You may find that outside of your Team Day, there are elements of daily meetings you need to hold with your team. And if you don't have a marketing department yet, there may be additional daily marketing elements you'll want to address. Maybe you don't need a whole day for Public Relations, but you want to be available for media interviews, so you'll want to plan that element. And don't forget your buffers so there's extra time available for a meeting you know runs over frequently or an activity that might need a little more attention to be done to the best of your ability.

Then it is essential to have some 'me time', something that you do just for yourself like sports, meditation, yoga, reading, etc. Choose whatever element nurtures you and gives you energy. A lot of business owners, especially in the first year or two, have a hard time slowing down and not constantly working. The thing is, that leads to burnout and a decrease in creativity and productivity, so this element doesn't just make you happy, it also makes you a sharper entrepreneur.

Then there's the element of a great life. Let's not forget, we do business to create a great life for ourselves and create conditions for a great experience. Having a great life might mean date nights, weekend trips, adventures with your friends, with your children – with whoever is essential in your life. Enjoy it. Remember that life is short. Make it count. If you want to do that, you must put it in the calendar, otherwise it won't happen.

> *Celebrate progress every week.*

Step 3: Add time blockers to your calendar

Now, we're going to take your daily intentions and the elements of your business activities and put them in your calendar for the Ideal Week. This way, you get out of the mentality that everything has to be done today, and you will be confident that you have time for the things that are most important. There will also be some moments of truth for the elements that have no space in your Ideal Week. Maybe they get delegated or outsourced or pushed to the future. In other cases, you may decide those elements are things you're going to say a hard 'no' to. How freeing is that?

To get started, use the Ideal Week template I referred to earlier, which you can find through the link at the end of this chapter, or start an Excel spreadsheet and create this calendar yourself. Put your five daily intentions into each of the five days of the work week, creating a column for each day. Also, decide what time your workday begins and what time it ends. Those are going to be boundaries you stick to, so that you have space to do things with the people you love and the activities that make you happy.

Then, for all the elements of your business activities that you listed, start colour-coding and collating them by type. I use a system in which activities for sales and growth are blue, which for me signals freedom, like the blue ocean. I put team activities in yellow, because those are fun and crucial. My 'me time' is almost clear, because then I'm invisible to the business and take a time out. Elements that I don't enjoy and are not CEO activities are shaded in red. My great life activities are green because they give me life, like nature. Locate my sample of daily elements through the tools resource link at the end of this chapter and notice how I colour-code them. When you have colours selected for your elements, start scheduling them in your days, considering which day's intention that element falls under. Your sales elements should mostly land on the Sales Day, and so forth. While my Team Day is almost entirely yellow, I also have yellow elements throughout the week, like our Daily Huddle.

The wonderful thing about this process is that you can test different things as you create your Ideal Week. What might it be like if you don't take meetings before noon? What might it be like if you only have sales calls on one day? You'll find new time opening up, which you can use for other elements that may have been on the backburner, like overhauling your employee onboarding system – things that you know need to happen for growth to occur, but you've been so overwhelmed with everything else that you haven't made time for them.

Once you have a good mock-up of your Ideal Week, compare it to your actual calendar. For most business owners, I bet they look quite different. Make a list of the elements that don't fit into your Ideal Week that have been taking up your time. Once you have this list, put them into groups. Which things can you delegate or outsource? For each, create a plan to hand over those elements. Which things can you pause for now and maybe return to when it's a better time for you? Schedule a reminder for yourself to reconsider that project for the next quarter or even the next year. Finally, what's left that's been taking up your time that you're going to say a hard 'no' to?

Make a plan to exit those things, whether they're deals that are bad for you, failed enterprises, unfulfilling relationships, etc.

Here's a mind-blowing tip: if you want a four-day work week, simply choose a day with that intention and book yourself up with me time. Even if you're not there yet, just seeing it on your Ideal Week will help you envision a plan to get there and will tell you what you need to say 'no' to if you want this to happen. Maybe that's a bit ambitious for where your business is now, but you can also challenge yourself to stop working an hour earlier. What can you say 'no' to and make that happen? Or maybe you want to work a half day on Fridays? Use your Ideal Week to create that lifestyle.

As you move into implementing your Ideal Week, return to my Daily Flow system from Chapter 5. I pair my Ideal Week with what's actually happening each real day by using the GTD method I mentioned. So, daily I list my top 10 projects and choose three tasks to make progress on those projects. Each day then has a goal of three activities to be completed.

Step 4: Respect your personal energy patterns

There's the ideal, and then there's reality. Most business books skip this part of implementing any new system, but it's important. My Ideal Week is not a static enterprise that I created once and then tried to religiously follow no matter what. It's a living, breathing idea that's flexible and changes with me and my business's needs.

To keep tabs on what's working or not working with my Ideal Week, I review and update my projects. I remove projects that are done from the week, as well as the ones that are not running well. I discontinue them and update the list. Remember those elements that you want to return to in the future? As I remove one project, I replace it with one of those waiting for time to open it on my calendar. I've always got a next project ready to kick off as I finish one. This keeps my business growing and scaling at a robust pace, and you can do the same thing with this system.

For your amusement, I include a snapshot of my actual first week of being a business owner with colour coding in the Action Tools section accessible at the end of this chapter. You'll see what it was like when I started my first year at Strategy Sprints. That calendar is full of fulfilment, fulfilment and fulfilment, which is in red. Every day the intention was fulfilment. Then, when I tried to have a great life in the evening, it didn't always work out.

My family missed me. On Friday afternoons, I tried to update my project list just to have a little bit of control over my week, but I had no power at all. Basically, I was trying to get as many clients as possible to make them happy by coaching them. But of course, I was also in the IT department and then every department because that was the first year when you create and found or build the concept of your business.

It's okay if you're in the first months or year of your business, and this is your reality. And if you've been running your business for a while without making many changes, I bet you haven't been growing or scaling like you'd hoped. This activity will show you why. What's eating up your time and stopping you from gaining traction on new projects? It's important to see where you are and then make a plan to grow into something that makes you happier. These changes don't happen overnight, but one thing at a time, you can create your freedom.

For me, once I started the team meeting and onboarded coaches to do the fulfilment that was previously on my plate, by my second year in business the week started looking better with less time spent on fulfilment and more time on growth and sales, which I render in blue. This is what I recommend for every business owner. Do less working *in* the business to do more working *on* the company. Create time in your calendar by getting out of fulfilment. You do this by training other people to do fulfilment, which means you create fulfilment systems that can be replicated without your presence. With your fulfilment systematized, you have more time for sales. Then, you create a system of scripts and expectations for your sales process and train people to do that, too. Then, you have time for more growth and CEO activities. You know the drill now, right? You create systems for those activities, and I have reached a point of delegating elements like joint ventures, collaborations, affiliates, and franchises because they are systems that can stand on their own and be completed by others without me in the picture.

By my third year of business, I wasn't doing any fulfilment and filled my time with sales, growth, and Top Three projects – not to mention lots of time to enjoy my great life. Even today, I continue to play with my Ideal Week. In some months, I return to tune up our sales systems. In some months, I stay completely out of that work. You'll notice that my day always starts with my Top Three activities that relate to my most important projects. I have protected that time so those activities will definitely happen. Every day. I also include my morning routine and 'me time' by doing things that are good for me. I do them early in the morning before I have breakfast with my kids because I have small kids. This will probably change as their needs change, too. Make room for the people in your life and their needs. Those relationships are everything and ultimately why any of this matters. Create an Ideal Week that fits your real life.

So, we start out trying to replace the red with blue, and then over time, you'll find that you can replace more blue with green. That's when being a business owner truly feels like freedom. Notice how there's more white for buffer time and green for great life on my fourth year's Ideal Week, as you can see in the screenshot at the Action Tools link at the end of this chapter. In the fourth year, I was entirely out of sales and had a lot of buffer time. For instance, you see that on Monday, there's a big gap between my Top Three and Growth. This allows me to give extra time and attention to those big projects, and it also makes room for any emergencies so that surprises fit into my Ideal Week.

Always remember… if you don't have time, you don't have priorities. Define your traction, so you know what your distractions are. You either work on your priorities or the priorities of others. You have to create time to create the system; to work on the business, and not in the business.

Final thoughts

Use your Ideal Week to create room for building systems around your processes. Without this tool, you and your business will likely burn out or stagnate. We don't want that at all. So, map out your Ideal Week so you can visualize the lifestyle you want. Look at what elements in your business exist now, and which should be there in the future so you can create traction. Block your time and use a colour-coded system to see if you're making the right choices about how to spend your time more and more as the CEO. When you respect your personal energy and allow your Ideal Week to grow and change with you and your needs, you'll create the business owner lifestyle you were dreaming of when you started your business. If you're wondering how to create systems or which systems you should create first, that's all in Chapter 7. Keep reading.

ACTION TOOLS

strategysprints.com/tools

CHAPTER SEVEN

Value ladder

As a business owner, would you describe yourself as 'productive' or 'busy'? If you're not sure how to answer that question or don't like your answer, let's look at why that is. If you're implementing the Strategy Sprints tools consistently, you should see that you're creating impact and then leveraging that impact every week. The goal of the Ideal Week exercise in the last chapter is to help you do fewer activities than you did last week. Otherwise, to move forward faster while you're doing more work to create that speed, you risk giving up the freedom that you wanted when you started your business.

In many cases, at this point, our Strategy Sprints clients will say something like, 'But it is complicated in our case'. I bet it is. Every week, many business owners deal with complicated situations. And after implementing the tools in this book, those complications become simpler and easier to manage. The less complicated a problem is, the more efficiently it can be handled or delegated.

Complicatedness only creates friction, confusion, fog, slowness, and lack of alignment. On the other hand, we want *complexity* because it creates a whole array of transformations. For example, something that is simple but complex is a guitar. A guitar is very simply made with a few elements, but it can create a vast array of sound in moments of experience.

On the other side, something that is overly complicated yet not complex at all is a Rolex watch. This watch is extremely complicated to build because it is made of many parts, and they must fit properly together. As a result, the complicatedness is high, but the complexity is incredibly low.

This complex watch can only tell you if you're on time or not on time. That's it. The variety it creates is just one thing; a measurement of when you are at a particular moment in time. In contrast, the guitar is quite simple with only six strings, yet it can create 100,000 sounds. This is the difference between complicatedness and complexity, which psychiatrist Ross Ashby coins as his Law of Requisite Complexity in his book *An Introduction to Cybernetics* (1956). We want complexity in our output, but we want to reduce complicatedness in our business structure.

If you want to simplify your business and create calm and peace throughout the whole year... then you need help when it comes to fixing the mess. Many business owners tell me they think their problem is not enough clients or not enough sales. Sometimes those are exactly the issues at hand, and in other cases, something else is broken or missing. Here are some data points for the four areas where I see business owners facing too much complication:

- Unable to link data to touchpoints (such as *Where are today's hot leads coming from?*).
- Unable to attribute value to touchpoints (such as *Don't know which marketing elements are bringing in good customers*).
- No automation, all manual processes (such as *Can't rinse and repeat activities*).
- Inadequate cross-team cooperation (such as *sales team, marketing team and ops team all working in silos*).

These complications make it difficult to measure your sales and marketing efforts or to know what's working or not. To grow your business faster, it's smart to shortcut the effort and time it takes to earn the trust of your audience.

That's where the Value Ladder comes in. A **Value Ladder** is a line-up of offers that increase in price and value. Each step on the ladder meets people where they are on their journey to become a customer or client – from initial brand awareness to the top-end decision to buy your highest-price offer.

Marketing your product or service is way easier if you have this Value Ladder in place. It's an effective way for you to build trust, maximize the lifetime value of each customer, and move away from the 'commodity model' of selling your services. So, the ladder reframes your service from a position of value instead of focusing on the price and treating it as a commodity. On the topic of value, I've seen that people don't buy your product, they buy what they can do with it. In other words, the reason the company thinks people buy is not actually their reason, or the value the company sees is not the value the customer perceives. With your Value Ladder, you build it from the perspective of the customer so that your messaging matches their perception. Design your business in a way that makes it easy for you to communicate, deliver, and improve it regularly, as we do at Strategy Sprints when we work with service-based businesses.

Many service-based businesses have 15 or so different services and have no idea which are selling better or are harder to fulfil, much less if they're priced at an optimal point. That's because the offers are too complicated and need to be simplified. Less like the Rolex and more like a guitar. We achieve this in five steps to create your Value Ladder:

Step 1: Define your Main Product.
Step 2: Describe the Sample.
Step 3: Know your Winning Channels.
Step 4: Have a Main Upsell.
Step 5: Include a Continuity Offer.

By following these five steps, you will create a tiered process that goes from your smallest offer to the Main Product, then to your biggest upsell. Then, I show you how to quickly create a sales page to start bringing leads that will want to climb the ladder. Follow along in this chapter as I explore all the elements of the Value Ladder. Follow along with the digital copy of the Value Ladder that you can print and fill out or refer to at the tools link located at the end of this chapter. Grab your pen or pencil, and let's do it.

Define your main product

To create the Value Ladder, you must decide which offer is your Main Product. Many business owners will argue that there's no way to know which offer is the main one, but the data will tell you. The first thing the Strategy Sprints coaches do with clients is analyse the revenue streams. In your financial numbers, you'll find the hard truth about which offers are selling better than others and their profit margins, along with the feedback scores for customer happiness with the results.

The Main Product is the one with:

1. the most impact on your client's results;
2. the one that is missed most by people who don't have it; and
3. the one that is most relevant to your buyers.

Those three components point towards the high perceived value on the part of your customers. Often, these most valuable offers require a bigger financial commitment that equates to more value and bigger results. To accomplish this, the Main Product must solve a significant problem and give them the transformation you've promised and that they're looking for.

We break down each offer according to the four criteria below, referring to the calendar app I mention in Chapter 2. Let's measure and compare the offers:

- **Avatar:** Describe who it is for. Remember to be extremely specific and go nine levels deep, as I discuss in Chapter 1. Ex. *Busy teacher and parent* et al.
- **Problems:** What are the three main problems that this offer solves? Refer to Chapter 2 for the villains you identified. Ex. *Want more time with family, less work stress.*
- **Deliverables:** Identify the top three ways you can solve the main problems, again using Chapter 2 in your solutions brainstorm. Ex. *Simple tool for time management, ten minutes a week saves them hours.*
- **Pricing:** With your expenses, what do you need to charge for this to be profitable, and at a number your customer will gladly pay and value? Ex. *The offer performed best at $10/mo., with a 30 per cent profit margin.*

As you compile your data for each offer, you'll notice which ones are out of step with the rest. For instance, an offer for a single avatar, which doesn't match up with any of the other offers. There may be others where the problems and deliverables might be combined so that there are fewer offers to cover the same problems and results.

Pricing is the most liberating and the most challenging phase of the exercise because finding the perfect price is difficult for many business owners. Sometimes they are afraid to raise prices in case people stop buying, and in other cases, the prices are arbitrarily high and don't match the perceived value of the offers, so people don't buy. Avoid all those issues with my pricing system. I teach Sprinters that with every new client, you raise the price by 5 per cent.

'Until when? Do we raise the price forever?' I am commonly asked. I say, as soon as you hit 40 per cent non-buyers. Track your sales call conversions, and you'll know if you talked to 10 people and 6 people buy. This means you need to end raising your price because you've found your sweet spot.

Some offers that underperformed might perform better at higher price points, and others you may decide are not worth it to continue. That's a great sign that you're making CEO decisions and simplifying your business. Ideally, you want to land on an offer suite with a Main Product that you'll showcase in most of your messaging to create rapport with your best customers.

The time-saving benefits of having a Main Product are life changing for business owners. Imagine you're only trying to market one thing instead of more than 10. You have more time left over to continue improving the sales, service, and customer satisfaction for that offer instead of trying to sell many things at once and creating a confusing message for your audience.

Describe the sample

What's happening when meal preparation subscriptions offer one week of free or deeply discounted meals? They give customers a taste to make them want more. This is the same thing that happens when a consultant offers a one-hour paid discovery and then invoices the client for a project. Even apps often give users a free taste of the functions and then offer paid, in-app upgrades. Now, we create this magic leap from the taste to your Main Product.

For the Main Product you choose, the next decision is to find what goes on the ladder before the Main Product, on the rung just below at the level of experience. You're looking for a way to give customers a sample of this offer so that they get a taste of how you solve the problem and want more help. This is working backwards from the offer, rather than building the ladder from the ground up. That's because if you don't know where you're going, it's hard to build a ladder to get there.

How can they sample your offer? Think of the Sample or taste as the smallest thing you can offer that allows them to experience the magic of your deliverable. For us at Strategy Sprints, this Sample is an audit. With Your Game Plan Audit, we can show both how we work and where we are experts, through the quality of our questions. For other businesses and industries, you may find that your Sample is a proof of concept or diagnosis. The Sample should be low-cost or even free for the customer, which means it should be automated or involve minimal time or work for you or your team. Sometimes the taste is a small investment so you and they can find out if there's a perfect fit.

When they buy your taste even for a small amount of money, you are triggering micro-commitment from your clients, filtering those people who will likely buy your other offers further up your Value Ladder. Without giving a taste, it can be difficult to turn marketing traffic into paying customers. People want and expect to try something out and see how it works or what the experience is before making a purchasing decision. Do this well, and your taste will sell the Main Product for you.

Know your winning channels

With your taste selected, which leads to your Main Product, then you want to decide how to drive traffic to the taste. Let's look at your current marketing channels to determine which one or ones are best for this taste.

Consider all your marketing channels that are sending you clients or customers regularly. These might be channels like:

- personal network
- YouTube
- LinkedIn
- Facebook Group
- Facebook Ads
- Google Ads
- membership community
- email marketing

For each channel you get clients from, consider which ones give you more quality leads. Which is a medium for you to get potential clients consistently? Also, which mediums are where your Avatar frequently spends time? If the customers will be at the beginning of the awareness stage of your brand and your Main Product, position your taste as a no-brainer so they can decide if they want to keep climbing your ladder.

In the calendar app example I mention in the Define Your Main Product section, maybe they find that running ads in apps and paying for placement in app search results are the best marketing channels, which might be expected, but then unexpectedly they also get a lot of customers from a free Facebook Group for parents that they participate in. They might also see that their YouTube ads aren't performing well at all and should be cut off and maybe revisited later. That's crucial information.

Also, you get to decide who you invite to the next level, too. Your Main Product isn't for everyone. It's for the smallest number of people who are the perfect fit for you. Otherwise, you are wasting their time and your time trying to solve problems they don't have or with solutions that don't fit them. That will tank your feedback score and not be a good fit for someone to continue climbing your Value Ladder.

Only put your marketing efforts into channels that are winning and stop wasting time on channels that aren't the right fit. This gives you more time and ad spend (if that applies to you) to devote to where your biggest, best leads are coming from so you can find more great customers just like the ones you have.

Have a main upsell

Now that we've built the bottom three steps on the ladder, let's look upward at what comes next after the Main Product. It's the Main Upsell, an offer that solves and puts a full stop to your customer's biggest challenge. This is the most effective solution your clients can take as a shortcut to achieve their ultimate desire. And it's usually more expensive than the Main Product because of its increased value.

To choose this upsell, identify your customers' biggest problem you want to solve. Also, include a concrete set of deliverables that will help them go through the process seamlessly and achieve significant results by implementing a straightforward strategy. Go wild with your imagination. If price was no concern for the client, what do they really need, which you can offer?

Maybe for the time management app, an upsell could be access to a help desk and a 30-minute set-up call with someone who would create the calendar for them, and that might cost much more than the Main Product. Or you could build out new features the Main Product lacks and then charge accordingly for those upgrades.

In some cases, you might create a ladder that allows customers to go from the taste to the Main Upsell. That's what Tesla does. Each model of its cars has a Main Product and then there is a Main Upsell if you want the performance version of the car, which increases the cost by $10–20K. In this way, Tesla doesn't add barriers to prevent customers who want the Main Upsell from selecting the higher price to get all the benefits available.

The price for the upsell is generally higher than for your main product, as the upsell is more comprehensive and more advanced. It can be in the form of a done-for-you service or a one-on-one set-up. Your Main Upsell is the perfect entryway towards a higher level of client that will push you to be a higher-level business and business owner. And for the customers who will love this offer and gladly pay for it, you are the answer to their wildest dreams.

Include a continuity offer

There will be two paths you can offer customers who love your Main Product and want to keep climbing your Value Ladder. Those are the Main Upsell, for clients who want even more of your help and more results, or for clients who want a continued relationship but not necessarily increased ways you can help, you can point them to your Continuity Offer, which is an ongoing or complementary service or product that continues to help them solve their problems. And provides you with recurring revenue for as long as they continue with this offer.

Once you have a customer for your Main Product, the business owner's question becomes, *how can I make them stick around?* For any business to grow, it's no longer enough for you to sell your services once. Instead, businesses need to think of ways of adding reliable, consistent sources of recurring income. And that's where continuity offers come in. And they come in different forms. For example, customers come to your business for value and results and stay for the community. This works in the airline industry when a customer comes to them for a flight but then stays for air miles and credit card points.

After your Main Product is delivered, what else could you offer to your customers by way of ongoing support? Look at your old list of offers from Step 1. Is there something from that list that wasn't a fit for the other rungs on the ladder that might work here? Usually, the Continuity Offer is lower in price and value than the Main Product, but it might only be available to current customers. It can be a subscription, a monthly call, access to continued teaching and training, accountability, etc. Your Continuity Offer helps people to stick around and be in your orbit.

Without a Continuity Offer, you watch happy customers exit your business a little confused that after this wonderful experience with you, that's it. Or you keep them happy and keep them paying you. When you have done that, you have your Value Ladder.

The 80% ready page

Now, let's get some qualified leads to climb your ladder from the Winning Channel to the Taste. A lot of the time, once businesses have a good Value Ladder, they fumble the sales process and scare the leads away before they are ready to buy. What if you can avoid all that and instead warm people up before you offer them anything? In this section, I show you how to get your leads 80 per cent ready to buy so you or your sales team can easily close them in sales calls. The idea is to make people ready to buy right before you talk to them.

The reason a lot of salespeople aren't closing enough calls is that they're talking to people who aren't ready to buy. Maybe they watched a video of yours on YouTube or commented on one of your social media posts. Then, they say, 'Okay, I want to speak with you.' Often, these people are not ready to buy, they're just interested. That's good, but it's not the right time to give them a conversation or a demo.

Instead, we want to take the people who may find your content and become, for instance, 10 per cent ready to buy. At this point, you need a process in their customer journey to make them 50 per cent ready, then 80 per cent ready, and that's when you offer the sales call. You should be talking with them when they're 80 per cent ready, not before. If you talk to everybody who is 10 per cent ready, you will spend much time persuading them to do business with you. They'll ask about the features and want to see examples… you can easily lose six or seven hours on one client who decides to wait and doesn't buy right then.

My answer to this issue is The 80% Ready Page. When someone sends you an email or message on social media and asks for a call, your next step will not be to send them a calendar link. You will send them to your 80% Ready Page to make them a hotter lead. Guess what goes onto this page to warm up the lead... it's *value*. We teach our Strategy Sprints clients to build value on an 80% Ready Page with a few key elements, including:

- Social proof
- Objection handling
- Trust building

Very often, these are the missing pieces between someone being 10 per cent ready to buy and 80 per cent ready to buy. And when you fill in those gaps of information, you bring the leads that much closer to saying 'yes' to your offer.

Social proof comes in the form of testimonials. These are valuable because they show the prospect a picture of your avatar that they will identify with if they are a perfect fit for your offer. This way, you and the prospect don't waste each other's time getting onto a call only to realize it's not a fit. If you don't already have testimonials collected, go back to your best customers and ask them for a few sentences about their happiness with your product or service and ask their permission to publish those words, along with a headshot and including their credentials, if possible. There's no substitute for letting your happiest clients speak in their own words and sell your offer to people just like them.

You don't want **objection handling** to happen during your sales calls because that is a bit late for them to find out if your offer isn't right for them. You will waste their time and your time speaking with each other if all they needed to ask is:

- *Okay, which project management system do you use?*
- *How does this feature or that feature work?*
- *Is it comparable to my system?*
- *Is it integrated...?*

Answer your frequently asked questions on the 80% Sales Page. If you don't already know what those most common concerns are that people bring to sales calls, ask your sales team for the most-asked questions. Bullet-point your benefits and features so they can skim and find the information they need to make a buying decision.

Trust building is about showcasing your expertise. Often, when a prospect finds you online, they will think, *Can I trust these people, or are they another internet guide trying to sell something? Do they have real results?* You partly answer this question with social proof, and the other piece of the puzzle is establishing your brand as a trusted source of credible information and results. Include details like a bestselling book, TEDx talk, logos of media outlets where you're quoted or interviewed, education or certifications, endorsements, etc. It's not necessary to have all of these elements, but consider what proof you have of your expertise and then make sure it's easy to spot on your 80% Sales Page.

The point of this page is not to make a sale, so the Call to Action is not to purchase. Now, it's appropriate to invite the reader to apply for a sales call and fill out a form. You or your team will review the applications and offer calls to those who are a good fit and give referrals or resources to those who are not a fit. Once you build this page and incorporate it into your processes, measure the responses from the applications and the rates of sales from those leads in comparison to your old system. You'll probably find that fewer sales calls are booked, and more sales calls are converting into sales.

Final thoughts

This Value Ladder really changes lives and our businesses by making them simple and uncomplicated business models. It starts with deciding what offer you're going all-in on with your Main Product. Then, you work backwards to create the Sample experience that will make them want the Main Product. Consider what Winning Channels are the best for sending you leads to accept the taste. Then, we build up from the Main Product to the Upsell Offer for higher-end clientele. You also want a Continuity Offer to keep happy customers engaged with your community and your brand in a recurring revenue model. In this way, your business is the guitar that makes 100,000 sounds instead of a watch that only tells the time. Fill in the gaps with your 80% Sales Page to bridge from social media to your sales calls. In the next chapter, I show you how to take this Value Ladder model and use it to create predictable sales.

ACTION TOOLS

strategysprints.com/tools

CHAPTER EIGHT

Predictable sales and reaching people more

Imagine this. You wake up in the morning with five sales calls on your calendar. They are 100 per cent the right people you should be talking to because you have an established filtering system that determines whether they're in or out (with the 80% Ready Page from Chapter 7). You have the first call scheduled when they are 80 per cent ready to buy. Calls are so effortless and all you do is offer the sale to them on the call. Plus, you don't improvise because you use a proven and tested sales script that converts prospects to clients consistently.

Sales team meetings are fun – not tiring and boring. Not only that, but the sales engine works even when you sleep or you're on vacation. While most business owners are waiting for three weeks to get reports from the month before, you have a real-time reporting system. You don't guess the numbers because you get them in real time. What kind of difference would that make to your business today? What about when the world gets shaken up?

During the Covid-19 pandemic, almost every business and industry felt at least a temporary disruption in their cash flows. Some businesses recovered quickly and adapted to the changes in their workplaces and supply or distribution chains. Others didn't recover well – or at all. From my viewpoint with Strategy Sprints, I noticed that our clients that were able to accurately forecast their revenue fared best. That was no accident.

When they knew what to expect from future revenue, they could make smart choices and adapt their businesses for hiring, research and development, commercial space needs, equipment, software upgrades, etc. In uncertain times, not knowing how much money you will have in the future is a recipe for making unhelpful decisions that could dig you into a bigger hole.

We live in an ever-changing world, so while 2020 brought the dangers of unpredictable sales into full focus, there are constantly unpredictable changes in technology and business dynamics that put business owners on a roller coaster ride. If you don't have a predictable sales system, in some months your revenue is $65,000, while some months it's $15,000; and you may not know what kind of month it is until the numbers are in at the beginning of the next month. That's stressful.

Then problems related to cash flow arise. If your cash flow is unpredictable, you don't know how much or even when you can afford to invest in growth strategies. At that point, you're stuck because you're always reinventing the wheel just to make things work. You don't have a proven step-by-step process to generate consistent results. In this case, each time a new project comes in, you create a new quote and new slides, etc. Quarter after quarter, you reinvent the wheel, leading to profit margin loss because you're investing too many hours creating new offers.

Another difficulty that can arise from not having a consistent process of generating revenue is difficulty scaling since you don't have a process that can be replicated. This means the work involved is so manual that you can't automate it.

I've got big news for you. To scale quickly, your sales system can run on its own like a well-oiled machine even without you (as the business owner) doing anything related to the sales process. To achieve this level of freedom, you need data to drive your sales strategy. Structured, reliable data is important in making critical business decisions, especially when building the next effective sales strategy to grow your pipeline.

One proficient process of monitoring useful data is through sales tracking, which is the process of closely monitoring and analysing the different stages of your sales systems. The purpose is to measure and quantify the success (or failure) of current marketing and selling efforts, and find areas we can improve or enhance. Sales tracking is vital because it provides precise information about your clients' buying patterns. It also helps to pinpoint their buying decisions and needs. Once you have a consistent process of tracking sales, you'll establish a predictable sales system.

A predictable sales system is an important part of your business as it dictates the growth or death of your business no matter what else is happening in the world or your industry. A predictable sales system is the best salesperson any business could ever have because it never goes on vacation or gets tired. It's sharp and ready 24/7.

In this chapter, I share all my best tools that our Strategy Sprints coaches implement with business owners to always know how much money is going to come in and make smart decisions accordingly. This includes:

- Sales Tracker
- Sales Estimation Numbers
- Scripts for Discovery Calls
- Ten must-haves of an effective sales script
- Seven stages of customer relationship management

Life may be uncertain, but your business's revenue doesn't have to be.

Sales tracker

To have predictable revenue, you must measure your sales performance and set targets so you can track how your actual results are measuring up to your ideal results. For example, if you want more clients, reverse-engineer what work you need to do to bring in more leads. Most likely, this means scheduling more sales calls. The more people you speak with, the more clients you have. How do you then book those sales calls? If they mostly come from networking, how many conversations do you need to have to get more bookings? This process tells me that tracking your networking output is important to predicting your revenue.

Our Strategy Sprints coaches start measuring the client's conversations, in this case to determine what their average amount is and then what their conversions are for setting sales calls and closing the sales to get a measurable baseline of their current growth patterns. Think of it like this. You count that when you have seven networking conversations, three turn into sales calls, and two of those become active clients, on average. So, what happens when you have 14 networking conversations? You probably double the rate of new clients, right? What about on a week when you only have four conversations? Predictably, that's unlikely to be a great week for growth.

Once you know your averages, start setting goals to improve those numbers with small experiments. Add a LinkedIn campaign or try Google

Ads and measure the results. Do your sales calls increase? Do those extra calls turn into customers at the same rate as your other marketing channels? Gather the data because you don't want to feel if it's working, the goal is to see it's working.

That's why I created a Sales Tracker for Strategy Sprints, which you may download from the link at the end of this chapter. We are big proponents of data-driven decisions, and you need to collect your data in one place to make those decisions strategically. I also suggest tracking reschedules for sales calls. When you look at how many scheduled calls never happen, you might also find room for growth. Maybe there's an objection you're not overcoming on your 80% Sales Page, which I discuss in Chapter 7, or maybe a certain marketing channel isn't sending you good leads. If you're not growing at a rate that you'd like to see, I guarantee the answer to why will be in your numbers. Use the Sales Tracker to find those leaks and plug them.

Sales estimation numbers

Your **Sales Estimation Number** is the composite of a set of numbers for expected profits, costs, and revenue that enables you to track the effectiveness of your business systems and processes. This number goes into your income statement, which is something you declare in Strategy Sprints. Imagine being able to say, confidently, 'this amount is what I expect this month.'

Month by month, you will get more accurate predictions of your Sales Estimation Number and go from volatile sales to predictable sales. You will trust that number more and more if you regularly update it from your Sales Tracker. And because of that, you'll sleep better and make better decisions because you can predict your revenue, like how to spend your money, in which things to invest, how much to invest, if you need to hire, who to hire, how much you can afford to pay them, etc.

Our Strategy Sprints coaches work with our clients to find their Sales Estimation Number using the spreadsheet available from the link at the end of this chapter.

The estimation is a formula that considers your sales pipeline, represented in the third column. Your pipeline may look different to this, so you will want to input your lead-to-customer milestones accordingly. We also notice your confidence level, which affects sales call performance. You update these figures each week to make your revenue forecast. As the weeks go by, a lead will move through these columns all the way to 'yes', or else they will call it off at some point along the way. When you're tracking that progression, you'll find areas of opportunity for where you can further optimize your messaging, processes, etc.

Let's understand where all these estimations come from. The first thing is to take stock of your sales confidence within a defined period. How high is your confidence rate that your sales calls will close in the next four weeks? If you think it's 0 per cent, then put 0 per cent. If it's 5 per cent, put 5 per cent. We like to start with an extremely low number and then increase it accordingly. At the other end of the spectrum, 80 per cent is being quite confident someone is going to buy in the next four weeks.

Next, consider the columns in line three of the Sales Tracker. The total leads include everyone at all the different stages in your pipeline. Then, you break down the leads by where they are in your pipeline. Qualified leads meet your ideal client criteria, and only enter this category when they've had engagement with you, such as expressing interest at a networking event, sending you an email to find out more, etc. Once they accept a sales call, they move through the pipeline to the scheduled call column. My business breaks the sales call process into two pieces, which I share more about in the next section of this chapter. In case you're wondering, at the point they give a hard no, leads should be removed from this count because they're not qualified. Of course, we hope more of these leads are getting all the way to your equivalent of a 'verbal yes'.

The next column looks at the potential estimated revenue that you could realize if all those leads become customers. Over the next few columns, you will track the potential revenue at each stage in your funnel based on the number of leads at those stages. This is to predict as closely as possible the number of sales next month, so if you don't like these numbers, use the Sales Tracker and find what part of your pipeline needs fine-tuning so that the forecast is more in your favour. If you see that there's only potential for less than half the previous month's revenue for scheduled calls, you can either see what qualified leads you should follow up with to increase those schedules or return to the top of your funnel to bring in more leads.

Scripts for discovery calls

In business, talking to prospects is one of the most challenging parts since you need to persuade them to part with their money in exchange for what you have to offer. And most of the time, business owners lack consistency in this area and sometimes find it difficult to control the conversation. A sales script is so important as this creates consistency and pattern because it gives you a starting point, it keeps you in control of the conversation, and anyone in the business can use it. For most businesses, the early scripts are created by the business owner who does most of the selling, and then later you create processes that allow a team member or set of team members to replicate that sales work.

In Strategy Sprints we have two call types for different stages in our pipeline. The Discovery Call is a 15-minute conversation we offer to qualified leads after they visit our 80% Ready Page. Then, from those calls we book a Demo Call, which is 45 minutes, and at that point we ask for the sale. This is a process that developed over time, beginning when I was answering the phone, which was, of course, not a particularly good system. It was no system at all. Nothing could be automated or delegated.

The first thing I did to create a system was to record the sales calls that I did. From that, my team and I tried to extrapolate:

- What is the checklist?
- What are the models?
- What are the tools?
- What are the steps involved?
- What's the magic there?
- What is working?

I watched the recorded call and took notes on a Google presentation to answer these questions, and in 30 minutes I created our first sales script that we tested with my team. At that time, we tried to convert prospects with just one single sales call. As we continued fine-tuning the script, we realized that splitting this into two separate calls worked better and that became our current pipeline process.

Discovery call

Two days before the Discovery Call, my sales team prepare by reviewing the lead's website to find out more about their current business. We use a specific template for that work to uncover:

1 What's their value proposition?
2 Who is the avatar?
3 What questions do we have?

For Strategy Sprints, a good lead is someone who needs help with their value proposition and probably doesn't have a well-defined avatar. In most cases, before working with one of our coaches, it might be unclear what they do or why a prospect should choose them. These are areas of opportunity to bring up on the call to see if the lead is feeling the pain from not having their message and positioning right.

In addition to doing our homework, we want to show up for the call as professionally as possible. Here's my checklist for pre-sales call checks:

- Ten minutes before the call, set yourself up in a quiet room to prep and take the call.
- Print the script and ensure your pen is working, as you don't want to make noise by typing during the call.
- Double-check the lights to make sure your appearance is professional.
- Select a background wall with your logo.
- Open Slide Deck (if needed).

All five of these practices were learned from experience and mistakes. Early in my business, sometimes I would work from a coffee shop, and if I sat near an espresso machine, my sales call would be interrupted by a macchiato. Hard to do a five-figure deal that way. I also noticed that if I typed during a call, the other person would stop talking – that was the opposite of what I wanted to happen. Also, in dim lighting, I had a harder time making a connection with the other person because they couldn't see me well. Sometimes my background had children's toys, and I found it easier to choose a green screen on Zoom, which has also worked well for my sales team. And when I needed to present slides, I could see the other person's eyes glazing over if I had to search my files to try to bring one up. This all had to be fixed in advance so I could conduct the calls with a winning vantage point.

During the call, the most important thing is to listen carefully to what the lead says. For instance, if they say, 'We want to go from $2.5 million to $3 million in revenue', don't immediately tell them what you would do to get there. Instead, ask, 'Why? What would change for you and your clients if that happens?' Then, listen for clues to a) What do they want? And b) Why do they need it? Go to the tools link at the end of this chapter and check out my Discovery Call template where I capture common wants and needs for the business coaching industry. Create your own version of this sales call form for your industry using our template. Then, during your calls take note of what they want (first row of boxes) and why it matters (second row of boxes).

To encourage the prospect to discuss these relevant details, ask questions such as: *What would change if you achieved this result? What happens when nothing happens to solve this issue?* These clarifying questions allow you to really understand their context and not just know what they want but also what they need, even if they don't ask for it. You're also reminding them what's at stake and showing them that you understand their issue and how important it is to them, already positioning yourself as the guide to lead them to their desired outcomes.

After the call, document your notes in their customer profile within your Customer Relationship Management (CRM) system. Include details like which offer from your Value Ladder is appropriate for them and what your next steps are. You'll also want to include any qualified leads on your Sales Tracker and place the expected revenue into the correct column and assign any next actions to yourself or your team to ensure a prompt follow-up for the next action the client needs to take to move through your funnel. Maybe it's a proposal they can accept, or it might be an additional call, which is what happens after the Discovery Call in my business.

Ten must-haves of an effective sales script

Now that you have a sense of the sales call process, let's go deeper into what you or your sales team will say on the call. Let's say you're a real estate agent, and a potential client sees your social media account and goes to your website where they download a valuable PDF that solves a problem for them about valuing property. In the follow-up emails or on the thank you page, that person watches your video that explains how you solve their problem on your 80% Sales Page. Then they are even more interested in your offer, so they click your button to schedule a call.

They're a qualified lead, and now it's your job to sign the client. Below I list the 10 must-haves of an effective sales script, which will be your North Star to make sure your calls stay on track and lead to a strong Call to Action (CTA) at the end:

1. Agenda

- 'Thank you for being on the call, and this is what we are going to cover today…'

This puts you in the driver's seat and sets the customer's expectations for the call, so they are less likely to try to take the conversation off-topic.

2. Qualify and diagnose

- 'What are the details of the project?'
- 'What are your ambitions?'
- 'What do you want to do?'
- 'What is your level of awareness?'
- 'What are your current numbers?'
- 'What numbers do you not know?'

This helps you and the client understand the scope of the work and what may be required. As you listen, begin to diagnose the issue by repeating back to the client what they say.

3. Contrast

- 'Did I understand you correctly? You have two properties. You are not using them. You would like to have this goal of XYZ in three months.'

As you ask each qualify and diagnose question, contrast where they are now with where they want to be to show them their gaps.

4. Benefits

- 'What would be the benefit if you do this?'
- 'What changes in your life?'
- 'What changes in your P & L?'

You don't talk about features right now, only the benefits – *more money, more time, more freedom, less waste, less headache, fewer costs*. This builds value in what it's worth to them to have their desired results.

5. Trial close (open-ended)

- 'Which one of these sounds interesting to you?'

The **trial close** is like watching your kid in a talent show. You are really bored, waiting for your kid to be on stage. When it's their turn, you are super awake. You take a photo. You clap. When the next kid is on the stage, you're bored again. Same here with the client's interest level in all your benefits. Now you show them the menu and ask them to tell you which benefits they are on the call to know more about.

And then you deep dive only into that one, otherwise you will bore them. That is the first trial close.

6. Deliverables

- 'We can deliver this cost reduction, this revenue increase, etc.'

For the benefit they are most interested in, discuss the deliverables. Deliverables still have no features. They are the milestones in your process to solve their problem.

7. Trial close (close-ended)

- 'Okay. Which one of these really interests you more?'

The customer will tell you exactly what they want to hear, and then you share that information with them. Only that.

8. Proposal

- 'Let's get you started on (deliverable) so you can (benefits). My fee is X.'

Now, you offer to work together. End this part of the script with your price. Then be silent for 15 seconds. Expect this to be awkward. You must shut up for 15 seconds after you say the price because now it's working inside them – the gap, the 10 times value, and the solution. This will create tension, making them solve it.

9. Close and objection handle

This is the moment where they will say, 'Okay, let's do this. How do we proceed?' Or they will let you know a question you haven't fully addressed yet. In that case, return to your qualify and diagnose questions to get clarity on the issue and then return to the trial close. Continue this process and keep the conversation going. Expect five to eight objections to come in one call.

10. Schedule a next step

- 'Okay, let's continue this conversation. I'm intrigued. Let's continue this conversation maybe in 10 days, 14 days.'

If you get to a 'yes', set their expectations. Are you sending a proposal by email? When should they check their spam folder if they don't see it? When will you follow up if you don't hear from them?

For calls that don't get to a 'yes', set their expectations, too. Ask for an additional call or another action that makes sense for your business. Don't wait a month for this next step. I suggest a week or two, so the conversation is still fresh for both of you.

These 10 components comprise the sales script. Keep a few things in mind as you put these steps into your sales calls. Calls rarely go directly to the sale. Often, it takes eight objections before you come to a 'yes'. Think of the objections as one door closing and another door opening because you want to understand them and help, and those objections take you closer to the close. You continue asking clarifying questions until there are no more reasons for them to refuse your offer.

This is the whole objection handling, and as you do more sales calls, collect the most common 10 to 15 objections your prospects have. Share those with your team to help everyone learn to overcome them with ease. I recommend that you run through this script at least 35 times with different clients to refine and improve your techniques. Around that point, if you wish, you should be ready to hand the whole system over to your team to scale the business.

A word of warning: if you hire a head of sales or salespeople before your script is fine-tuned, this delegation of sales calls probably won't be successful. Often, our Strategy Sprints clients will argue that 'I am not good at sales. I don't want to do it. Let me hire a salesperson. They will do it.' However, without an excellent script, how can you hire and train people for sales? The first things a good salesperson will say to you are 'Show me the script. Show me the conversion rate on your sales calls. Show me the recordings of good calls.' If you have those pieces in place, the salesperson has a starting point. Without those script essentials, only an inexperienced person would accept the position.

Seven stages of customer relationship management

> 'What if instead of *reaching more people*, we would seek to *reach people more?*'

This is a question I asked my Strategy Sprints team in a marketing meeting. We were brainstorming ways to bring in more leads to increase our projected revenue throughout our Sales Tracker. We were already doing a lot of paid ads on multiple channels, and those were optimized and performing well. So, how else would we grow this business and help more business owners?

Finally, with this question, we realized where else we should look for more leads – our own list. Wow. All our marketing and messaging was about bringing in brand new leads and warming them up, but we were practically ignoring the people who already received our email welcome sequence.

The customer relationship is a crucial part of any business. You make the most impact when you maintain the same quality of interaction with all your customers and leads. The way to do this is to build a system that will send this communication without overwhelming you and your team. We found that creating specific messages for customers at different stages of the Value Ladder from Chapter 7 would help us stay connected and engaged with the people already in our audience.

CRM is important in any business as it equates to an increase in profitability, productivity, loyalty, and customer satisfaction. Commonly, you'll find many kinds of CRM software, and different ones are appropriate for different industries and list sizes. HubSpot is the CRM we most recommend, and we also use Close.com. However, since software is always changing, this chapter focuses on how to be strategic with automating specific messages at appropriate places in your Value Ladder based on the client's actions no matter which CRM you choose. An effective CRM is composed of strategies, activities, and mediums to manage communication while building a certain level of relationships with current and potential clients.

If your CRM is set up with your customers in mind, it will strengthen customer relationships, resulting in customer loyalty and retention. Our CRM changed the way we work and eliminated some manual tasks entirely. And it helped us increase our scheduled sales calls and demo calls, which increased our sales without bringing in a single new lead.

If you are reading this book and haven't completed your Value Ladder or the Sales Tracker and Sales Estimator, create those tools first, and then you will be ready to implement your CRM. In this section, I share the seven stages we take clients through in our CRM:

Stage 1: Awareness
Stage 2: Nurturing
Stage 3: The sales opportunity

Stage 4: Closing
Stage 5: Delivery
Stage 6: Upsell
Stage 7: Continuity

Essentially, these stages follow the Value Ladder and consider at each point if the leads are cold, warm, or hot. The Value Ladder starts with *cold leads*. This means they are aware of us, interested, and have interacted with our brand in the past. Maybe they clicked around the website and found the 80% Ready Page, which then makes them *warm leads*. Then, they schedule calls with us. When that happens, they become *hot leads*. Then, they continue that cycle as you saw in the last chapter until they become a paying customer.

For each stage, different actions, templates, and processes are appropriate to encourage them to continue to the next stage. Giving a 'closing' sales call too soon will be much less successful than doing so after value-building. Start integrating all these pieces into your CRM to give each lead a personalized experience with robust outreach that is automated. At each stage, your CRM will tell you what you need to do next with every lead.

Stage 1: Awareness

We begin Stage One with a brand-new lead. In your CRM, input their contact information, name, business, and any other identifying details they provide. At this point, they are a **cold lead**, so identify that in the CRM profile. My drop box for leads qualifying includes the following and even more sub-categories:

- Awareness
- Nurturing and engagements
- Warm lead
- Unqualified lead
- Scheduled sales call but did not show up
- Completed sales call and didn't buy
- Became a customer
- Did not close
- Became a Superfan

The list follows the seven stages and at different times allows for different outcomes, like proceeding through the sales cycle or opting out at a certain point. More about this list as I discuss the stages.

With the lead entered into the CRM, then assign this lead to someone on your team or yourself to take the next action. Generally, when someone is just now entering your CRM, they will be at *Awareness*. Perhaps they filled out the contact form on your website, and the next step is to send this cold lead an email. Create templates to reply to leads that are in Stage 1 to take them from Awareness to Nurturing. Then, your CRM will automatically generate that Awareness email response. If you don't have templates for outreach, build them from the emails you're sending now to these different stages.

Stage 2: Nurturing

When the client replies to the email or I see that they took action by clicking a link from my email, I know we're in Stage 2, and they're starting to warm up to our brand. Often, I am asked, *How do you know what they are doing or who is doing it?* That's part of the beauty of a robust CRM. There is a tagging system in the backend to follow the client's actions, and you can automate what is sent to them next based on that action. You can use Zapier or IFTTT to connect your website with your CRM system and your email system for tracking action across your platforms. These two programs simply work by initiating a trigger, which causes another action to happen automatically. For example, when a visitor clicks three times on a PDF, we have automation to tag them as a warm lead. If a viewer watches 10 videos on our website from beginning to finish, we have automation to tag them as a hot lead.

So, when a lead does a certain action on the website, we clearly define what message is right for them at that point of engagement. Then once we identify where the leads are in the journey up the Value Ladder, we will move them from one point to the next.

My role or my team's role is to continue engaging with the lead to make them warmer. We accomplish this by sending the next email template that perhaps provides valuable content to increase their interest and activate them to accept a sales call. Always send nurture content with a call to action for the lead to respond or otherwise do something to engage with you. The more that happens, the hotter the lead will become.

Warm leads are a little bit interested and do engage with you, but not enough to accept a sales call. They need a little push to buy your product or service, such as being invited to visit your 80% Ready Page. So, you activate them regularly until they become hot leads and accept a sales call they book from that page.

Stage 3: The sales opportunity

When they become **hot leads**, we enter a potential new business opportunity because they have scheduled a sales call. This means you enter the client into the Sales Tracker. From here, the lead's status can go in many directions, such as: Hot Leads, Abandoned Audit, Qualified After Audit, Did the Discovery Call, DC No Show, the DC was done, Did a Demo Call, Did Become a Customer, Did Become a Referral Source. Have templates ready in your CRM for all those possible outcomes after someone schedules a call with you.

The lead may cycle through these different sub-stages before you arrive at the moment to ask for the sale and get them to 'yes'. Be patient and continue considering what stage the lead is in and what value is appropriate to share with them next to keep them engaged. This is where you can lose a lot of hot leads in a sales pipeline if you send lots of contact before scheduling the sales call, and then once you have the call or have spoken with them, you ghost them if they didn't buy on the first call. That can happen out of fear of reaching out too much or not knowing what to say and, of course, fear that they will say 'no'. Use your Value Ladder to tell you what value you should be building for them, and after the first call, refer to your notes for what they need to know more about or what feelings you can address to bring them to purchase.

Stage 4: Closing

This is what all your nurturing and engagement is leading up to, the point at which the lead moves all the way to the end of your Sales Tracker and says 'yes'. Now, they are sold 100 per cent. Instead of a hot lead, they are a hot, new customer. Track this in your CRM by sending them the agreement and invoice or whatever the next steps are to make the sale and have them enter their credit card information. Now, automate a welcome email and set their expectations for what's going to happen next now that they are a customer.

You still want to track their activity and make sure they complete the payment and have automated messages to send friendly reminders if they don't complete the sale in a timely manner. Then, you might return them to a Stage 3 process. Assuming they do complete the purchase, it's time to give them the best customer experience possible.

Stage 5: Delivery

At this stage, you map the outreach to the client during the life cycle of the offer they accepted. This can look quite different depending on what the offer is. For a package of coaching sessions, you will automate things like appointment reminders and follow-ups after sessions. If your program follows a formula, you can automate the delivery of worksheets and tools to be sent along the timeline of the coaching.

For a single product, such as a subscription to software, this might trigger a sequence of emails that ensure the customer is benefitting from the tools and nurture them throughout the subscription to make them aware of new improvements and upgrades, as well as client wins to keep the customer inspired and engaged.

Services also have delivery processes that can be automated. You might automate weekly updates for the client to keep them abreast of your progress, reminders to give feedback after you submit the work, and appointment reminders and follow-ups for any meetings.

Stage 6: Upsell

Sometimes your hottest leads are the people already doing business with you. Think back to the opening of this chapter when I realized we needed to reach to our leads more, not reach out to more leads. One of the fastest ways to increase the numbers in your Sales Tracker is to move people from your Main Offer to your Upsell. You might automate this by setting a criterion for actions that people in your Main Offer take that qualify them for the Upsell.

Depending on what your Upsell is, this can look quite different. In some businesses the Main Offer may solve one problem, and the Upsell may solve additional problems that arise after you solve the first issue, such as after someone creates a CRM, they realize they need help with copywriting for all the templates. So, the Upsell is appropriate for customers making progress with the delivery and who may be ready for more help from you. In other cases, those clients who struggle to be successful with the Main Offer may prefer the Upsell. If the Main Offer teaches business owners how to do their own public relations, those who struggle with the course may prefer to hire your PR agency to do the work for them. Within software subscriptions, Upsells might be additional features or adding seats.

When you tag an Upsell lead, you may offer a sales call and move the lead into a sequence for selling this additional offer. Then, when they accept, you sign them up for the Upsell automated emails.

Stage 7: Continuity

In your Value Ladder, continuity is about accepting an ongoing offer for continued support, after the Main Offer or Upsell. Here, that offer would place the customer in receipt of the continued support. Stage 7 is about continuing the relationship with a lead after they say 'no' or get stuck in your Value Ladder by not taking action or after delivery is finished, and they are no longer a customer.

Continuity is priceless because a happy previous customer might refer someone else to you when you stay top-of-mind. This kind of opportunity can grow, as happened for us at Strategy Sprints when a former client expanded their network and referred a good number of additional clients to us. This customer became a **referral source** because they were so happy and satisfied that they talked about us well to their friends and colleagues. In the CRM, at the beginning of the funnel, I also recorded who they referred, so we have actual data on the continuity value of previous customers.

Those referral leads are not hot leads yet. But they are warmer than warm leads that come in at Stage 1 because they trust the people who told them about you. There is trust established in that relationship, even before you meet them, so it's more likely that they will become hot leads. You can even build email sequences to touch base with leads that are referred and especially to thank your referral sources.

The art of the follow-up

The art of sales is in the follow-up. The CRM method is straightforward, but will you do it? For most business owners, this part is boring and easy to forget. I find that you do best with an inner helper and an outer helper. The sales are in the follow-up, and I need 8–14 conversations to close a high-ticket item. That's internal for me to motivate myself to keep having those conversations. Then, externally I have the AI reminding me who to follow up with. This can also be a personal assistant or a routine team call to go through lists of leads and their status. Even with a team, it's important to keep a personal touch in your follow-up communication and show yourself to be of service instead of looking for the sale like a robot.

> *Stop selling. Start serving.*

Final thoughts

Start predicting your sales with the Sales Tracker and Sales Estimation Number so you have your goals set and can measure your results. Create a sales script with all 10 of my must-haves that you or your team can use, so you can get more clients for your business. This will build consistency of results, creating a domino effect on your revenue in the long run as you continue to scale the business and move from being the CEO to the owner. A CRM is an excellent tool to systematize your process and strategies in cultivating communication while building and nurturing relationships with your current and potential clients. It's also a great way to increase business efficiency and profits as you track how you move leads through the seven stages. To top it off, this automation will industrialize your sales process and ties together your Sales Tracker and Value Ladder to free you and your team from manual, repetitive tasks so you can work on higher order concerns, such as measuring and increasing client feedback, which I discuss in the next chapter.

ACTION TOOLS

strategysprints.com/tools

CHAPTER NINE

Feedback is the breakfast of champions

If I can choose between happy clients and successful clients, I take the latter. In fact, I'm more successful when I forget happy clients.

> *Forget happy clients.*

Maybe that seems a little counterintuitive to you, and it often raises eyebrows from coaching clients as well. Here's a recent conversation about feedback.

'I sent out a survey asking my clients if they are happy with our service, but only 1 per cent answered,' said the client. I was on a call with him after he had sent a customer satisfaction survey to his Software as a Subscription (SaaS) subscribers.

He was worried because only a small number of his paying clients answered the survey, so he wanted to know what he did wrong to get so few responses. *Did they not like the software enough to reply? Did they hate it so much they don't know where to start?* As a result, he was afraid of asking for feedback a second time. He worried that nobody would answer the second time they asked, which would make him feel even worse.

And then I asked him a question: 'Does your client treat you as a trusted partner on their journey – a partner of their success?'

'Oh! I never thought about this,' he said. All his attention was on adding features and making sure his code was bug-free. The idea that he already had or should have a 'relationship' with his customers was eye-opening. His software was contributing to successes, but that didn't mean the users naturally saw the correlation. He agreed to create more personality-driven, story-based content and then try again to do a survey the next quarter.

In your business, your customers need to treat you as their business partner. Otherwise, they will not give you feedback. Consider that 'partnership', in the truest essence of the idea, is about sharing information to grow together. When you are perceived as a partner in your customer's journey, they will tell you more about themselves and their experience with your brand because they want you to understand them better.

And the more you understand your customer, the more you can improve and adapt your business to match their needs. In cases where your customers are not sharing information, they treat your survey as a task and not a way to give a partner information, which was the case for my client.

Feedback, or lack thereof, speaks volumes about how your customers treat your brand when doing business with you. The key here is relationships. If you're a mere supplier or a service provider, you can be replaced by someone else in an instant. Just like in marriage, you need to work on the relationship for it to grow and flourish. Establish a strong foundation of trust so both partners will be genuinely interested in meeting each other's needs.

> *Feedback is the breakfast of champions.*

Feedback is a two-way street. The more you give it, the more you get feedback in return, and you need to get that feedback to continue giving it. To make this happen, start by giving your customers a reason to trust you so they share feedback, which allows you to know how you can provide the best service for them.

One reason my clients are reluctant to ask for feedback is a fear that it will be negative, and perhaps you feel the same way. However, even if everyone answers your survey with 100 per cent positive responses, that feedback would be meaningless to you. Remember that I opened this chapter with the idea that we're not looking for happy clients, but successful ones. And to help your clients win more, you need to know where they're not winning now. If they say:

'Your product or service sucks!'
'You didn't meet my needs.'
'You're not good enough.'

that's okay because this is invaluable feedback in business. What's more important than how they feel is how you approach it when they tell you the hard truth. Do you just avoid the truth given right in front of you and blame user error? Or do you take action to solve the challenge? Just like in a marriage, if you avoid answering the difficult questions, the relationship may eventually come to an end.

Be proactive. Show that you're open to letting the other partner know about your point and work together to make things work for both of you so your relationship will grow and last. By talking, giving each other feedback, and adapting based on that feedback, your relationship will become more meaningful, and the foundation of trust will be rock solid. That's why it's important to think about the relationship between the brand and the client. You start by asking your clients the right question to serve their best interest:

- Are we doing the right thing?
- Are we still on track?
- Are we meeting your needs and expectations?
- What other things do you need that we're not covering yet?

Once you know the answers to these questions, you have a clearer idea of the overall health of your business. And knowing the overall health of your business is important as it translates to growth in the long run, which you can measure by inputting your updated feedback scores into your Growth KPIs, which I discuss in Chapter 3. Your feedback is one of the top five numbers to track, measure, improve, and becomes the internal benchmark of your continuous improvement process. In this chapter, I'll show you how your feedback score can improve the way to ask clients for feedback and the way you act on their feedback to raise their success and your score.

Understand what your clients really need

We collect and collate feedback as a benchmarking tool to gauge customers' satisfaction towards your products and services, including the overall experience around your brand. Our process is inspired by the Net Promoter Score method designed by Fred Reichheld, a partner at Bain & Company. He discusses this idea in *The Ultimate Question: Driving good profits and true growth* (2006). Essentially, he says the goal of getting customer feedback is to address the relationship, needs, and especially unmet needs between you as the brand and what you offer to the client.

Your feedback score also translates to how likely customers are to recommend your brand to their family, friends, and colleagues. It is calculated by asking customers one question: *On a scale from 0 to 10, how likely are you to recommend this product/company to a friend or colleague?* Data from this question helps businesses improve their service, support, and delivery to increase customer loyalty. Based on the survey responses, you'll determine the feedback score.

The responses are grouped into three categories of customers:

Superfans (score 9–10) are loyal enthusiasts who are happy to keep buying and referring others, fuelling growth. These are your raving fans.

Neutrals (score 7–8) are satisfied but unenthusiastic customers who are vulnerable to competitive offerings.

Unsatisfied (score 0–6) are unhappy customers who can damage your brand and prevent growth through negative word-of-mouth. These people are unlikely to buy from you the second time and may even encourage others not to buy from you.

For my analysis, an ideal feedback score is around 60–70. If you have that rate of feedback, your business is more likely to thrive because you don't only have happy clients, you have raving, happy clients who tell their friends about doing business with you. So, they become your brand ambassadors marketing your business for you, as you can see in Figure 9.1.

FIGURE 9.1 Superfans that market your business for you

A couple of hundred or a couple of thousand people pointing straight to you is the most helpful thing the business can have because brand ambassadors are proof of impact – proof that your services are helpful.

There are many platforms and survey generators that offer ways to collate this feedback, but you can also do it manually if you don't have a large customer list yet. Conduct your one-question survey, and then use this formula to get your feedback score:

> Number of Superfans *minus* number of Unsatisfieds *divided by* number of responses.
>
> Take that number and *multiply* it by 100.

That's your baseline to track your feedback.

Now, for whatever your score is, no matter if it's high or low, it's important to understand how to use it. Let's just assume that you have equal responses of two each across Superfans, Neutrals, and Unsatisfieds. For most companies, this would be a good opportunity to see the NPS at zero, which means you have room to move the Neutrals and Unsatisfieds up to Superfans. For you to get a feedback score of 25 per cent, you would need two ratings to shift to either 9 or 10. Twenty-five per cent is not bad in the first place; getting to a 60–70 per cent feedback score is quite difficult to achieve.

No matter where you start from, look for ways to move more customers from Neutrals and Unsatisfieds up to Superfans. Identify the little tweaks and experiments you can try, then keep measuring as fast as possible to determine which changes are positively affecting your score. The goal is to achieve 60 to 70 because it's the healthiest position you can have when it comes to your business.

This is one of the numbers in our weekly Strategy Sprints tools, and it should be part of your team discussions for continued improvements. When your feedback score is quite high, it also becomes effective marketing material because other customers will be attracted to highly rated products and services.

Calculate feedback the Strategy Sprints way

As you already know, feedback is a powerful tool that leads you to dive deep into growth opportunities to improve your customers' experience related to your product or service to retain them and turn them into brand ambassadors.

The more specific feedback they provide, the more you know exactly what you want to work on for your short-term projects. You know exactly what's working right now, and what areas you need to double down on.

In our case, Strategy Sprints is a 90-day experience, so we ask our clients for feedback every 30 days. This means that for the duration of the programme, we ask them three times. Because our onboarding is evergreen, different populations of customers are hitting those benchmarks every week. We send an automated survey weekly to the customers at those milestone moments in the journey, and the next stage is manual. In our business, we update our feedback tool manually because we want to feel it and be intentional with this measurement. Download your copy of our feedback score system through the link at the end of this chapter.

In addition to the referral question, here are some others we ask:

- What's going really well?
- What are you missing?
- What do we need to improve?
- What else do you need to do that we are not delivering right now?

As you collate this feedback, categorize it according to where the customers are in the journey. So, for me, it's helpful to measure how many responders are Unsatisfied or Neutral at the 30-day mark to see if those scores increase at 60 days. Or I may discover that something is wrong with fulfilment if the score drops, and more customers are Unsatisfied or Neutral at the 90-day mark. If you have more than one product or service, also track which offer the customer is responding to. An additional thing to track for each offer and stage of the offer is the percentage of customers that respond. Radio silence from a large portion of your customers likely means they're not Promoters, and you'll want to engage with them more to build a relationship so that they will respond to you.

In my business, our response rate is always 100 per cent. That's likely because we're asking one-on-one coaching clients for responses, and they have good partnerships with their coaches. Also, they answer because it is in their best interest to help us continue to shape our offer to best fit their needs.

But sometimes you want to ask a broader set of people for feedback, as with my SaaS client I opened the chapter with, and those are customers with whom you don't have a direct day-to-day connection. If that's the case, then the percentage becomes relevant so you can also track how your efforts to build a partnership are working to encourage more feedback.

I've also seen coaching clients ask about following a number I wouldn't track – your industry standard. One big misconception that many people have is to benchmark your business performance against other companies. That is a waste of time and energy because you don't learn anything helpful for your growth forecast. For example, I could compare my business that has a 64 per cent score to other industries like Apple, which has 75 per cent, but that is not an apples-to-apples comparison. Or I could compare 64 per cent to another business coach that has 35 per cent. My score is higher, but so what? If I don't know why my clients rated me higher and that coach lower, this difference is meaningless.

So, we only compare ourselves to our team's performance from the previous week. It is not important if you are at 76 per cent or if you are 26 per cent. The important thing is that if you are 26 per cent today, the next week you should be shooting for 27, and this way, every week, you become better than last week.

Win big with your feedback

Every seven days, I watch our feedback numbers come in and want to see an upward movement. Otherwise, we need to improve our product, experience, onboarding, and some part of the fulfilment. The goal is to increase the trajectory. To keep increasing that score, we continue to face the reality of how good our customers tell us the product is now, what to improve, and what to double down on. But we don't only focus on the Unsatisfieds and Neutrals, we also celebrate the Superfans.

With every Superfan, you can potentially add three more clients with this last survey question: *On a scale from 0 to 10, how likely are you to recommend this product/company to a friend or colleague?* For those 9 and 10 responders, follow up soon and ask them: *Who do you know that needs our service? Would you introduce us?* In this way, your feedback loop also serves as a referral system and the product improvement system at the same time.

Final thoughts

It's important with such a small effort on your end to send a feedback survey to your customers. The impact on any business is highly significant as you build customer relationships that increase retention and referrals. Plus, it only takes five minutes a week to update your numbers and stay on top of your feedback. By doing so, we are increasing the feedback score of the business one point at a time. In the next chapter, I show you how to create more impact with less time and effort in your marketing.

ACTION TOOLS

strategysprints.com/tools

CHAPTER TEN

The seven elements of marketing

My company had a couple of rough years with marketing when we entered the digital ads marketplace. To be blunt, our Facebook Ads had zero impact. Month after month we spent money on the ads and tried to change the images and the copy, but nothing seemed to help. We were also producing content on every platform we could think of, yet there seemed to be little engagement, and my team was spread thin trying to be everywhere and do everything. Although I had made key hires in marketing, ultimately it was my task as CEO to create a success plan the team could follow.

It seemed like everyone else was winning with these marketing channels except me. That reminded me of my wakeboarding experiment. I had thought it would be cool to ride a wakeboard and ski on the back of a boat. It sounded easy enough, so I bought the equipment. I expected to step onto my board, for the boat to start, and then I would glide through the water jumping onto waves like a champion.

Well, instead the boat started, and soon I was holding on for dear life. It was tougher than I thought to hold onto the handles – and staying upright? Forget it. I just hoped I wouldn't lose my expensive board. This was embarrassing because I'm an athletic person, and I'm good at sporting activities. To make it even worse, I had friends who were staying upright and jumping like naturals. I was wondering why some of my friends could do it easily while I failed miserably… which was the same thing happening with my Facebook Ads.

I discovered I was lacking enough strength in key areas of my body that I needed for stability. And I hadn't devoted time to learn the techniques for choosing waves and how to position yourself to jump at just the right moment. The list of reasons why I failed at wakeboarding is quite long. The point is, I was not concentrating on the right things because it was a hobby, not a passion. I was trying to excel at too many sports at the same time just to have fun. So, I cut back and focused my time and attention on my favourite sport, running, and let go of my wakeboarding dream.

I wondered if my marketing efforts were suffering for the same reason. I had invested money, but not strategy, and I was trying to win at too many things, so I was a generalist in all the platforms instead of a specialist. This lightbulb moment led me to simplify our marketing and create a system that produces better results to grow and scale profitably with less effort.

> A successful marketing system is about… fewer activities. More impact.

It was freeing to decide the solution to my problem wasn't to be better at everything but instead to laser into the marketing channels and strategies where we would apply our ad spend and focus. In this chapter, I share the Seven Elements of Marketing that create more impact with less effort:

1 Positioning
2 Traction channels
3 Reusable content pieces: articles, testimonials, and calls to action
4 Email automation
5 Retargeting ads: Facebook and Instagram
6 Unique mechanism
7 Irresistible offer

With these seven marketing elements in place, you will be strategically positioned to grow and scale your business by attracting highly qualified prospects and turning them into clients.

1. Positioning

The concept of positioning is about branding and messaging, but to get those right, I begin with distinguishing your business in the marketplace so that you know who you are and what you want to be known for. From those decisions, everything else becomes much easier. Recall Chapter 1 when I shared the Blue Ocean Strategy for being unique instead of vanilla? That's about one thing: differentiation as you create your blue ocean where you're #1 for your specific thing. The basic idea is to become the best at some parts of your business and let all the other things be your competitors' fields in a sea of red. Those parts where you choose to excel become your uniqueness criteria, and ideally, they will correspond to the things your best customers are looking for. For me with Strategy Sprints, my uniqueness criteria include *speed, implementations, price, tools, community, moderation, team building, and analysis.*

Once when I was teaching this to a client, they said, 'But Simon, you have a quite strong community in the entrepreneurial field and the private equity field. You are the guys with a great community. Why isn't that one of your differentiators?'

I said, 'Because I know we are not #1 in community.' Having a community that is alive, healthy, interesting, and creative doesn't mean we're the best at it. If we decide to go for #1 in community, we will stop building other aspects of the business and put much more effort and energy into community. The clarity of what we are best at and are not best at is our positioning.

Have you considered the #1 differentiator you want to be known for in your industry? Take a piece of paper and refer to the tools linked at the end of this chapter. Find out what the buying criteria are for your customers, and those elements are where you shoot for #1. Let the other components go to your competitors. With your positioning chosen, it's time to choose your traction channels.

2. Traction channels

Most business owners that work with Strategy Sprints coaches come to us running a business with at least 12–14 marketing channels. They're doing things like paid ads, organic content, JVs, etc to hopefully bring qualified leads into their worlds. I term those avenues for leads 'traction channels'. However, they're not all created equally, and we find that in most cases, our clients are making the same mistakes we were in the story that opens this chapter. Trying to win in too many places, they're spread thin and winning nowhere.

If you have more than 10 traction channels, minimize the number so you can become an expert in a few platforms. I find that the sweet spot is five traction channels. If you have five working channels, you don't need anything else to win with your marketing, and growth becomes about scaling what's working, not about adding new channels. If your business is brand new and your problem is no channels, start with two traction channels and then when those are working for you, go up to three and so forth.

Here's why. Do most business newsletters and social media posts feel fun? I don't think so. When you focus on just a few traction channels, you differentiate yourself in those places with amazing, seemingly effortless content because you're not grasping at straws. You know from your own experience what works for you, and you do that. This makes your business and brand feel different.

As you choose your traction channels, keep your attention on qualified leads. Do not track the fancy KPIs like hours that people watch YouTube videos or total followers. Those are metrics I was measuring that are not important to scaling and growing your business. The important thing is how many people click the call to action and say, 'I want more of this'. That is one qualified lead. Another useful metric is the percentage of opt-in users that interact with your PDFs. Are those people accepting your next offer on your Value Ladder? Those are qualified lead behaviours you want to track so you know if your traction channels are working well. And those metrics will also help you develop reusable content pieces.

3. Reusable content pieces

Another problem my business used to have was constantly coming up with new ideas for content. We would create a post or article that performed very well with views and actions taken, and then we would go back to the drawing board to create something else that would be as popular or more so. This was exhausting and wasted a lot of time.

We found success with Gary Vaynerchuk's 'The Gary-Vee Content Model'. The core idea is that you can create one piece of content like an article and reuse it in many spaces up to 8–10 times. To implement this process, our Head of Marketing, Michelle, created our 'assets refinery'. She came up with this name to describe how our three content creators (she, Alexander and I) work together as a bank of knowledge that our content assets like emails and articles are based on.

The refinery begins with the monologues I do once a week, which come from my idea bank I keep on my phone, augmented with the interviews we do every day. Michelle will prompt me to choose a topic on Friday. On Mondays I write a draft that I mostly outline, and have our copywriters bring that writing to complete and conduct an editorial review with Michelle. When she's satisfied, I get final approval before publishing.

Every article on our website is reused in the newsletter of that week, as well as on LinkedIn. Then I record a video based on the topic, and sometimes I also draw on my iPad as part of the video. Mattia, our video editor, then cuts and edits the recording into several videos that Michelle publishes on YouTube. Then, the best videos are further clipped into highlights and shared. Then at the end of the week, we have an email newsletter again based on the week's content.

For videos that bring a lot of qualified leads, we reuse them as a free lead magnet on our website. For very strong content, we also add it inside Sprint University, a comprehensive platform where we host our different programmes. At other times, I create a Skillshare course out of a core idea.

If you're wondering where you'll find the time for this, I would say I put in two hours per week. The rest is up to my team to manage their time to get the deliverables in place on schedule. However, this assets refinery is meant to be created and then continually repurposed, not to infinitely create more content week after week. In our experience, it is enough to have 15 articles, 10 client testimonials, and five Calls to Action (CTA) and you will have infinite content to repurpose.

Calls to Action are opportunities to turn traffic or viewers into subscribers and get them into your Value Ladder. Here are some examples:

- Click here to get a FREE Report on Business Growth and Scaling.
- Click here to get the guide on this topic 'How to do lead management the best way'.
- Click here to do a short audit and to find out how much cost-cutting potential there is in your company.
- Click here to have the first free online course on this topic that interests you.

So, to put it all together, you create articles and share snippets on the topic across your five traction channels, always with a CTA to bring marketing leads into your business. And once they accept your CTA, create email automation to give them a compelling onboarding experience.

4. Email automation

Nowadays, it is easy and cheap to have a great email automation tool and to build a so-called 'funnel' to nurture your leads. Relationships that nurture new leads create fast exchange and value with your customers. I break this section into nurture emails and launch emails, which you will want to think about differently.

Nurture emails

Maybe you've noticed that most marketers don't seem concerned with the relationship part of their automation. Just today, I was told by a CEO that he's bombarded with offerings in his inbox and would never accept them. 'I don't like the way they do it. They don't know me. They come in and they want to talk about whatever topic I never showed interest in. They immediately want to sell something, and I would never buy something from somebody who wants to sell from the first shot.' His criticism is right, but what if email automation isn't in your face trying to sell?

Think of the relationship with each new lead as it would unfold over real time in person. Traditional marketing tells us that it usually takes seven to nine touchpoints before a customer buys something, like a hamburger. If you go to a fast-food restaurant, the decision was taken because of seven to nine contact points. Maybe you woke up in the morning and heard a specific burger ad on the radio. Then you drove to your office and heard it again. On the drive, you saw a billboard with a burger. After work, you wanted something to eat in a hurry, and you saw the exact burger again. Then you thought, 'there's this place that has this burger'. Now after these contact points your mind would say, 'I will go and eat that burger'.

It looks and feels like an intuitive decision to buy the burger, but it is not. It was built up over the whole day. Now, this is how marketing creates desire by creating a relationship and installing many, many different touchpoints.

But not every company has the budget for or even needs jingles or billboards. Email automation helps you create brand awareness with a tiny budget. There are platforms that charge as little as $50 or €50 per month to automate a series of emails to deliver when someone opts into your Calls to Action. Just send a very respectful message with exciting topics that are relevant to the kind of people that would want a particular piece of content they signed up for. That is the power of email automation. Notice the strategy I use: if someone accepts a CTA for productivity, they will get an email series on that topic, not on strategy or growth.

Launch emails

'What is the perfect launch?' I get this question all the time, and it's one of the ones most asked of my Strategy Sprints coaches as well. When you're launching, you have a new product or service to offer. Most marketers focus on grabbing attention at the very top of the funnel, often because they might be paid for the number of leads acquired. Others only consider the sale, especially if they're paid a commission based on sales. Both approaches overlook the most important part of a launch.

I learned from Google about 'The Messy Middle' in their article, 'How people decide what to buy lies in the "messy middle" of the purchase journey'. They note that marketing is not linear in the online space. They explored the question, 'When do people really make buying decisions?' and they were surprised that buyers were not so much making instant purchases. Buying choices were more about exposure and then a set of triggers that led to the purchase. I experimented with many of the types of triggers they identified and created a core of triggers that can be tracked to convert leads into customers: one feature, immediacy, scarcity, testimonials, credibility, and free or risk-free.

In a launch, most likely your triggers are going to be in the form of automated emails. It can be so scary to create funnels, and often clients say, 'Wow! The funnel is so overwhelming – 200 emails going out, and all these behaviours to track.' Email automation can be complicated for beginners, so I created the following list of eight essential emails for your launch.

1. THE WHY

In this email you grab the reader's attention with why your content matters to them. After all, that's why they accepted your Call to Action.

Write an email that answers these questions for the reader: *Why should I care? Why does this matter?*

If you have testimonials from your customers or language from reviews of your offer or that of a comparable competitor, use those to make the reader feel like you're inside their head speaking their own deepest thoughts to them.

2. DIRECT VALUE

Immediately give incredible value. For example, you might share one chapter of a book or one PDF that helps the reader do budgeting or a five-minute video that helps them decrease costs in a smart way.

That's directly giving value. You're giving away something valuable for free so it's more than you are comfortable with, and this can inspire the recipient to feel reciprocity and want to give back to you with taking more action or even a CTA for a sales call or purchase – when the value is fully built and the relationship is nurtured.

3. THE BENEFIT

A lot of marketers are so excited about their features that they forget what the customer cares about most – the outcomes for them of purchasing and using the product or service.

In this email, paint a picture of their vision of what it will be like for them when they have the benefits of your offer. Consider the Hero's Journey that I mention in Chapter 2 when writing this email and ask yourself these questions: *Where can your offer take your clients to help them on their journey? What's the promised land? What does it look and feel like to them?*

This future-pacing helps them imagine their reasons to want to say 'yes' to your offer.

4. THE LIFT

By the third email, readers are more discerning about whether to keep opening them or not. It's important to keep the reader engaged because now you're getting to the middle of the launch. In the middle, you must keep the energy high.

Consider writing an email about a story of somebody who used this product and it changed their life, or an uplifting example of what's possible for your clients.

Consider using dialogue to keep readers engaged.

5. THE PROOF

Demonstrate how you deliver on your promise: share how it works, with facts, details, and real results. Here's what I mean. It's not enough to claim, 'We helped 100 people have a better team experience'. Instead, feature one person with a name and professional title saying, 'Our client satisfaction increased by 14 per cent using [name of the product]'. Even better if you can get a high-quality headshot to include. Be precise here. This email is about proof, which is the difference between successful launch emails and all the blah blah blah out there.

It's good also at this point to have something visual, such as a video, image, GIF, etc, to keep the energy of your emails high.

6. THE OBJECTION

It is really key to proactively talk about and overcome objections. Put the objections on the table and discuss them openly. This is to your advantage because your leads are thinking these things anyway. When you bring them up and give a satisfying answer, you remove a lot of barriers between your offer and the customer's 'yes'.

Some common objections you might consider include: not enough time, too expensive, not good enough quality, and too risky. For example, now your lead might think, *Oh, but this is expensive.* Then, you have an opening to say, 'If you invest 15K in this product, you can get 73K out of it, and here's how.' Look at your data about objections and your scripts for overcoming them in your sales calls for inspiration about what to write in this email.

7. THE CLOSE

Now you're ready to move the reader to action. The CTA needs to be clear. Give one button. There is one thing they do, and the objective is either to book a sales call or buy from the email via a checkout page.

If your offer is below €2,000, a low-ticket item, it's usually fine to invite leads to purchase straight from the email. For offers above €2,000, high-ticket items, you probably need to get them on a call to close the sale. I find that it often takes one or two calls to close high-ticket items.

8. LAST CHANCE

Make sure no one misses out with this final email that concludes the launch. Here you introduce scarcity, which people will tell you they don't like. Neither do I as a receiver. But according to the Google study, saying 'this is your last chance before the offer goes away' significantly drives people to make a purchasing decision.

These are the eight essential emails. For more advanced email marketers, check out my free tool with the link at the end of this chapter for an extended 14-email sequence, which focuses more on overcoming objections by reframing beliefs.

5. Retargeting ads (FB/IG)

Retargeting is a powerful tool. For example, when a visitor lands on your website, you can retarget them with ads when they're on Facebook or Instagram. My approach is to run retargeting ads for 45 days after someone has visited my site. That is a good window of time to stay top of mind if they are still deciding whether to work with me. Also, these leads are warmer than cold leads you can also target but haven't been on your website and most likely have not been exposed to your brand before. Those are harder to convert into customers than people who already know at least a little about you and have already sought you out.

When you're running ads, consider the **Customer Acquisition Cost (CAC)**. The CAC is not a vanity metric. It's an effective metric to know how much it cost you to have that Facebook Ad to book five calls. And out of those five calls you have one client. What is the monetary equivalent behind that? How does it fit your profitability and revenue scheme? What ad spend does it take you to book the five calls that result in one client? What if you increase your ad spend to book 10 calls and then acquire two new clients?

6. Unique mechanism

If you're looking for new clients and you're competing with other businesses in the same market, then you need to offer something that your competitors don't have. You need what Todd Brown calls a unique mechanism,[1] which is a feature within your product or service that shows how it works to provide the promised outcome or claim. The unique mechanism solves the problem, delivers the promise, and elicits the results.

For example, Strategy Sprints offers an audit for our unique mechanism. You can create a video, infographic, survey, audit, eBook, free mini course, etc to show this proof of your offer's outcomes. When choosing your unique mechanism, notice what only you have to offer and create a Value Ladder from the smallest component to the next one leading up to your Main Offer. This small teaser of what you do immediately creates value and builds desire for more of what you have to offer.

Add scarcity and urgency when you make your unique mechanism available. If you say, 'Usually the [unique mechanism] costs [X], but now it's free for a limited time period', more people will be inclined to accept it. And you have an opportunity to prove your integrity when people ask you after the deadline if they can still have the free offer. Tell them, 'Sure you still can have it for free when I run the deal again in September. Or you can pay and have it now.'

Now you create a loop of attention and scarcity.

7. Irresistible offer

My first boss was an excellent manager and salesman. He told me, 'When you create a product offer, it should basically sell itself because of its clear value.'

It went like this: 'You get offer stack valued at €75K, and you only pay €7K.' That was an irresistible offer because with so much potential value, customers would pay a lot of money. That is basically an offer that sells itself.

For Strategy Sprints, we broke this strategy down into repeatable elements that everybody can do anytime. Check out the Irresistible Offer tool available from the link at the end of this chapter. You'll see how we score the nine elements of an irresistible offer using the scorecard you can fill out for yourself, considering your current offer or one you want to offer. Here are the criteria:

Pain of customer: The first box to check is whether we understand the pain of the customer and not just the needs. I measure this by my confidence to finish this sentence for my customers: 'I cannot sleep at night because of...'

Specific solution: This consideration often mirrors your positioning and the blue ocean you create where you are the champion at just a few solutions.

Benefits: Benefits are not the features. Here, dig deep for the hidden desires your offer can awaken, things like freedom and making an impact. Some people's deep desires are time and revenue.

Results of the offer: Refer to your tangible outcomes and deliverables, as well as your defined promised land and the vision of what it can be like for your customers after they benefit from your offer.

Value: The secret to creating value is to diminish the risk of the investment. Consider:

- How much is it worth?
- What is the risk?
- How can you reverse, giving me a guarantee that if this value is achieved then you pay if the product doesn't achieve that?
- Is there a value included that they don't pay for?

Often, your best value creation is to completely reverse the risk with a 30-day money-back guarantee.

Positioning: Refer to your work earlier in this chapter for your Blue Ocean Strategy where you're in a sea of one as the obvious choice for your target client.

Social proof: This is as simple as providing a quote from people you've worked with or your customers using the real words they say about you.

Warm up: Get them to 80 per cent before the offer using your 80% Ready Sales Page.

Squash objections: Handle the common objections even before the offer. This means answering the questions your prospects would ask right before it happens.

Now, fill out the scorecard for your offer and add each score to tabulate the total. A 90 would be a perfect offer score. Work towards that goal. For now, look at any element where you scored less than a 10. Why? Also ask for feedback from your team and customers about how your offer is really doing and what could be improved to make your offer more irresistible.

Most businesses will need at least a second round of this offer evaluation. Do the second round of testing. Whenever you arrive at the sweet spot when it comes to the price of your irresistible offer, then it's time to increase the price.

You'll know that your offer is irresistible when the revenue goes up and the conversion rate of your sales increases.

Final thoughts

There are only seven elements you need to successfully market your product or service to your target audience. Position your brand as the best in just a few key areas where you will stand out as the uncontested champion. And it's time to stop trying to be everywhere and focus on five traction channels to keep your marketing strategic and engaging. Use the same content over and over with reusable content pieces to save time and build authority faster. If you haven't yet, embrace email automation and use my simple launch email sequence to increase your 'yes's. Use retargeting campaigns to find warm leads for paid marketing channels and offer a unique mechanism that will be in high demand. And don't launch without pressure-testing your offer with my nine elements to make sure it's a no-brainer to your customers. In the next chapter, I go into even more detail about your content assets to help you quickly build authority and grow your brand.

ACTION TOOLS

strategysprints.com/tools

Further reading

Protheroe, J and Alistair, R (2020) How people decide what to buy lies in the 'messy middle' of the purchase journey, ThinkWithGoogle.com, https://www.thinkwithgoogle.com/consumer-insights/consumer-journey/navigating-purchase-behavior-and-decision-making/ (archived at https://perma.cc/TC2Q-KLEX)

Vaynerchuk, G (2018) The Gary-Vee Content Model, GaryVaynerchuk.com, https://www.garyvaynerchuk.com/wp-content/uploads/GV-Content-Model-1.pdf (archived at https://perma.cc/4F35-64FT)

Note

1   Todd Brown (2019) Does your product have a unique mechanism? ToddBrown.me, https://toddbrown.me/does-your-product-have-a-unique-mechanism/ (archived at https://perma.cc/4Y6C-R8R7)

CHAPTER ELEVEN

Your assets

Throughout this book, I discuss the importance of having a target customer and the right positioning. When you know who your offer is for and how your business is positioned, you answer two of the most strategic questions to grow and scale your business. These choices allow you to be different and then double down on what sets you apart from the so-called 'competition'.

With a clear, genuine, and appropriate foundation you are well on your way to grow and scale your business. Most business owners – even successful ones – don't have a clear answer to these two questions about who the customer is and what their marketplace positioning is, which leads to a lot of bad leads and poor sales. However, when you master these two elements, then you don't have competition – you have a blue ocean, as I discuss in Chapter 1. That's the point at which your offer appears to your best customers as the obvious choice, beyond compare.

> *Stay different. Stay you.*

By positioning your business as different, you present your unique combination of patterns and superpowers, so your offering is not comparable to anyone else. Your offer is only available to your target customer from you. If this is right for them, they will buy it.

My Strategy Sprints coaches help clients convey their positioning by helping them curate seven main assets for conveying their uniqueness across many different channels and platforms, and I break down how to create each of these assets in this chapter. The seven essential assets are:

1. The 30-Second Pitch that quickly grabs attention.
2. The 7-Second Tagline to turn internet browsers into customers.
3. Your uniqueness that creates and keeps your marketing ocean blue.
4. Your own phrase that immediately makes people think of your business.
5. Social proof with massive success stories that prove you solve the problem better than anyone.
6. Authority content so valuable you're seen as a leading expert in your field.
7. Professional platform that brings your assets together where the marketing magic happens.

These seven assets will ensure that your positioning is clear and that your message will resonate with your target customer in a way no one else's possibly can, whether you are networking in person or creating content to share digitally.

The 30-second pitch

You may already be familiar with the idea of a 30-Second Pitch if you attend business networking events that give a chance for everyone to briefly introduce themselves and their business. That is one avenue to use the pitch you create here, but also pay attention to the myriad opportunities you have when you're in casual conversations, such as at a professional conference, and someone gives you an opening to talk about your business. In that moment, you have 20–30 seconds to get and hold their attention. Most business owners squander those conversations and say whatever comes to mind instead of giving a strategic, memorable pitch.

Notice the positioning strategy in this simple, fill-in-the-blank sentence:

> [Target customers] work with us to get [desired outcome] through [unique mechanism].

Replace the bracketed phrases with what you would say for your business. For example, with Strategy Sprints I might say, '*CEOs* work with us to *create more time and freedom* through *simpler processes*.' I differentiate my business from other strategy advisors because usually, the strategy advisor only does business advice and doesn't also simplify processes. Processes are really operations and fulfilment. In our blue ocean of strategy advisors, we are implementers. It's not just about presenting slides via a distant relationship. We don't tell you how smart we are and what you should do, but we work with you on your spreadsheets and processes that are essential for your business. See how the 30-Second Pitch works?

Create a few versions of your sentence and try it out. Test it in your email signature and see what the feedback is. Also give it a shot as content in the body of your newsletter and see if you get more responses or button clicks.

Then, test it at network events and check the eyebrows – are they up or down? You want people to say, 'How interesting. Can you tell me more?' not 'Yes… interesting'. But what they really mean is that it is boring, and they quickly end the conversation. And even worse, they may say, 'I am confused. Now, what exactly is this for? Who exactly is this for?' Those questions tell you to refine the sentence because the target customer and positioning are not clear. You are looking for the perfect pitch that instead makes them want to find out more, or even better, put some time in the diary to discuss it further. Those responses indicate that you're nailing your positioning and your ideal customers get it.

To perfect your pitch, create several drafts and practise saying them, as well as sharing them and measuring the response. Continue to refine it until you have a sentence that's short and prompts your ideal customers to want to know more.

The 7-second tagline

The not-in-person equivalent to a 30-Second Pitch is the 7-Second Tagline. This brief statement grabs attention when people are scrolling the internet, so I like to describe a good tagline as 'thumb-stopping'. You might also see taglines on T-shirts, pencils and pens, and other promotional products. The tagline exists without you and should state your positioning and laser-focus on your target customer by itself, which is even more challenging than the 30-Second Pitch for most business owners.

To get your creativity going, let's learn from some masterful taglines I've collected from other businesses. Notice Domino's Pizza's tagline: 'Fresh, hot pizza. Delivered in 30 minutes or less.' If I see this tagline on an online ad, there is nothing else I need to know. If you are into pizza, now you know exactly what you're getting and how quickly. I also like this one from Verizon: 'Can you hear me now? Good.' This cell phone service provider escapes a red ocean of competition on price and instead emphasizes the quality of their connection. Let's look at one more from WP Engine: 'WordPress. Hosting, perfected.' That tagline is incredibly concise. Yet, the amount of information is quite high. You need nothing more to know exactly what you get. In each example I shared, in seven seconds, they get across the whole positioning and the entire offering.

Ready to create your own 7-Second Tagline? Here are some guidelines to create a strong tagline and evaluate if a tagline idea is perfect:

- It should be **simple** with only one main idea or thought.
- It should be **clear, not clever**. Sometimes people try to come up with very clever ideas that are usually a bit *too* clever and must be explained. You might feel good about the clever tagline, but for the recipients, it's white noise.
- It should be **clear, not confusing**. Look at how people react and do the eyebrows test. Are people confused, or are they interested?
- It should be **memorable** in the relevant context when people want to research it or decide to buy.
- It should be **unique** and not anything like your competitors.

If you already have a tagline, evaluate it using the above criteria to look for opportunities to make it stronger. If not, create something and start testing it. I don't expect you to master this in a couple of days. Tagline development is a process of months and years of experimenting. You start with one and improve it all the time until you get into the level of mastery that is impactful.

Your uniqueness

Once I worked with a car manufacturer whose vehicle price was much higher than other cars in its class. So, to create their uniqueness, we considered that maybe the goal shouldn't be to compete with the other cars. Instead, we looked to position that brand with small aeroplanes because the price was much more relatable to the planes. They started showcasing their cars at aeroplane events and found a warmer audience than they ever had at car events. This brand started winning more because they changed the landscape where they were competing, where they were totally unique.

I frequently see course creators making the same mistake. They think the competition is other course creators in their online niche. They overlook that they are competing against the vacuum where their target customers are trying to do the thing by themselves and struggling. To try to compete with major players – even when you are one yourself – is an exhausting order. Instead, you can make marketing easier by embracing your strategic differentiation and simply be one of a kind.

The goal is to become a market of one. Just like I did for the car manufacturer, consider *what market are you really in? Really?* And *who is really your competition?* At my client's price level, the people that might want their cars were choosing between that and a plane.

To come to this realization, we considered the key value factors in their customers' buying decisions so we could position their offer as the obvious winner. We determined that the people buying their cars chose them for luxury and status at an affordable price. That wasn't this car against another car, it was this car against a more expensive, less convenient, out-of-sight plane. Getting to this positioning was about deciding where to be weak and where to be strong. We want to be strong where the customer sees the most value and weak where we're not trying to compete.

Yes, I want you to choose where to be weak. Just as the car manufacturer decided not to even try to position themselves vis-à-vis other cars. There, they allowed themselves to lose, because they were winning somewhere else, where they were the only car that might be a better choice for someone else considering planes.

If it's not already clear to you what the key factors are in your customers' buying decisions, create a survey and ask some questions to find out, or you might look at your testimonials or sales call notes and see what they are already telling you. Your best customer is the one that agrees with you and says, 'The things you are weak on aren't important to me, but I absolutely must have the things where you are the clear winner. That's what I need.' They appreciate your uniqueness.

Your own phrase

Imagine you can reduce your tagline to have it on a T-shirt or other promotional product, which reminds your clients of your brand's uniqueness. Your friends also tell others so you can generate organic virality. When you get it right, you can have zero marketing spending and have the whole marketing game be in referrals because a powerful phrase can help you have a referral engine – a network of people who tell others about your business. You make it easy for them to share the phrase because it is simple and easy to remember in three to five words.

For example, what brand comes to mind when I share these phrases? 'Go Bananas with Free Email Marketing.' And then there was, 'Love What You Do.' They're also known for saying, 'Send Better Emails Now.' If you're thinking about Mail Chimp, you're right. They have done a fantastic job of continuing to coin phrases that catch on and increase their brand awareness.

As result, when people think about email marketing, Mail Chimp is often the first CRM that comes to mind. They're not trying to compete by being the best at a particular feature. Instead, they are banking on finding even more customers that don't really understand or care about the features – they want a culture. They want an online business, or an online aspect of a physical business, that's fun. That makes them laugh. As is commonly known, Mail Chimp got their very name from jokes about creating automation to do things you could hire a monkey to do. This CRM feels easy. That's what their customers value.

Brainstorm some phrases you could test that might catch on. Keep trying them out and notice which ones you find others saying back to you. That's how you know you just might have a winner. And like Mail Chimp, once one phrase becomes tired, have another one to debut and keep your phrase fresh.

Social proof

I was recently searching for a CrossFit coach. As a beginner in CrossFit, my intention was to find out who the best coach was and go with that person. The CrossFit database provides clear rankings, and I easily found the highest-rated coach and hired him. This was amazing social proof because I instantly knew which coach was most approved by more clients.

Even if you don't have an obvious platform to compete for ranking, consider the value of other ways your customers can support you, like public reviews. Look for places to list your business on Google, Amazon, Facebook, Yelp, etc and invite your customers to leave you reviews there. Having a high number of positive reviews is not a vanity metric like trying to get a certain number of followers. On the contrary, the more positive reviews you have on as many channels as make sense, the more credible your offer becomes to potential clients. And the more your reviewers seem like people just like the target customer, the more weight they will give to their peers' words. Also, take screenshots of those reviews and share them on your social media to get more traction with them.

In many buying situations, it's not as simple as being ranked #1 or going for five-star reviews. In those cases, you convey your top ranking in the most believable way possible – customer success stories and testimonials. These instantly build credibility faster than all the certifications, degrees, and boasts in the world. For customer success stories, you can write up narratives about how it was for them before they worked with you and the impact of their results afterwards. You can also ask the customers themselves to film a two-minute video describing this transformation. These stories tend to be longer than testimonials. A testimonial is just a sentence or two about the impact of working with you. Of course, always get permission before sharing your customer's endorsement and using their name or a headshot.

Additionally, you can create social proof with an influencer endorsement. If your ideal clients will know of and respect an influencer who will vouch for you, that endorsement can also increase your perceived authority. Do make sure if you go in this direction that the endorser makes sense for your offer. The right endorser can make all the difference, so when you work with an influential person, don't be shy to ask them to say some positive words about working with you and give you permission to share that testimonial.

One more note: when you hear other leaders discuss social proof, media placement frequently comes up. I think getting quoted or featured in magazines, newspapers, TV, and social media is overrated because in many cases, it doesn't directly correlate to a return on your investment. However, if you see an opportunity to be in the media, take advantage of it and be certain to repurpose screenshots and include the publication's logo on your home screen to increase credibility.

Authority content

Many business owners find content creation overwhelming because they try to follow advice about posting three to five times a day and either run out of ideas or burn out. If that was your experience, the truth is you don't need to create this much content. We've found that our Strategy Sprints clients do very well with at least 25 assets that are valuable and significant in their niche. So, this is about strategically creating the right content that builds your authority instead of being a 'content machine'.

There are many formats your authority content may take. It should be a combination of white papers, magazine articles, blog posts, PDFs, webinars, videos, etc. Consider how an underwater photographer could create authority content. They might start with a 15-page PDF called 'The Underwater Photography Guide'. Perhaps this includes some checklists, common pitfalls to avoid, social proof, etc. This asset might be available through your website's CTA as a free download, which will put users into an email funnel. Then, you might create a video about the information in the guide and post that on your website or other social platforms and link back to where people can download the guide. Here, the two assets are the free guide and the video, which work together to support your effort to find new leads.

As you plan your 25 content pieces, think of how they will support each other and all the ways a single asset can be repurposed, as I discuss in Chapter 7. Keep the topics to what you choose as the areas where you're #1 to your best customers and avoid discussing parts of your field in which you allow yourself to be weak. In this way, you build authority in your niche and become better known as the go-to for your blue ocean.

Professional platform

With your authority content created, you want to showcase those assets in a primary and secondary channel. A primary channel should be one that you own and control such as your website. For a secondary channel, I would choose the social media platform where you have the most engagement or know that your target customers also hang out there.

I see a lot of business owners who want to establish authority, and they do this by starting with secondary channels first, such as blogging platforms. The reason that's not the best strategy is simple: that platform can change, and you will have no control over it. They can change their algorithm, terms of service, etc and you could lose your followers with no way to get them back except to build your audience again. They could even change their hosting, and your content could disappear.

Take responsibility for owning your assets and publish them first on your website or blog, then put the assets on your secondary channel. What's on your website is yours, and what is on the other websites is theirs, so own your assets.

With your authority content published, then it's time to optimize and ensure that it creates value for the recipients. When you publish a piece of content, test it and measure the response. Get feedback from your audience and improve the content to make it more valuable and interesting to them.

Decide how often you will publish new authority content and be consistent across your primary and secondary channels. The topic of consistency reminds me of the film, *Burnt* (2015). It stars Bradley Cooper as a two-star Michelin-rated chef who wants to achieve the coveted third star. He has an interesting conversation about why he doesn't like the food at a particular fast-food chain. 'Consistency,' he answers. His issue is that they always put the same ingredients in the same foods. To him, consistency is not about always using the same ingredients. Instead (and I agree this is true for content creation as well) the consistency should be in the experience. You shuffle the ingredients to create consistent experiences that engage your audience.

Think about your authority content ingredients, such as experience, information, success stories, and the context of this piece of content. For context, consider if you're writing to address an issue current in your industry or to directly respond to something in the media, etc. You use those ingredients to create consistent experiences that continue to inspire and delight your followers, in the same way that a French chef will serve a new *amuse-bouche* in the hope that it will delight the diners as much as the ones that came before it. The chef wouldn't continue serving the same dish with no improvements. Reservations would decline, and the business would suffer. So, the consistency you're shooting for isn't repetition, instead it's innovation.

Here's an example from my Strategy Sprints assets. In 2019, we focused on two core topics for daily content: how to get clients and how to regain your freedom. A graphic designer created a series of five images for us that evoked those topics with our branding. So, we had two ingredients, the topics and the images, and we reused them for a whole year by innovating with an additional ingredient, like experience, success stories, information, etc.

Final thoughts

These assets are something to build up over time and continue innovating as your business and industry change and as you see shifts in your audience and what they gravitate towards. With your 30-Second Pitch and 7-Second Tagline you become memorable to the people you meet and who engage with your brand. It's also important to stand out with your uniqueness to be unforgettable. Adding a phrase can extend to brand recognition. Don't overlook the value of a positive review and use your customer testimonials and success stories to largely do the selling for you as social proof. Create authority content and post it consistently on your primary and secondary channels to elevate your expertise and become a go-to because your audience knows exactly where to find you.

ACTION TOOLS

strategysprints.com/tools

CHAPTER TWELVE

Hiring system overview

Hiring the right people has a significant impact on the success or failure of your business. That's why the hiring process should be given the utmost attention, the same amount as marketing and sales. Your business can't operate optimally if you don't have world-class people who will help you propel your business to the next level. Bring in world-class people who are passionate about the purpose that you're passionate about, and the whole business will become much more impactful.

I didn't always know this. I thought the goal was to attract top talent, period. So, when it came to hiring, I looked at optimizing my hiring funnel, which is a common way to try to make the best hires. Before the Job Scorecard, I treated the job posting as a hiring vehicle. In reality, it's much more of a marketing vehicle where you can show the soul of your company. My first job postings were boring and ineffectual. I would lose a lot of new hires within just a few months. It's customary to lose a small number of employees a year due to natural fluctuations, but I had many good people leaving after three months. This was happening after a lot of initial investment on my part. As they were often remote workers in all different time zones across the globe, employees would send me a video and say, 'Simon, this is not working…'. I didn't want more of these videos of people putting in their notice.

This brought me to Giorgio, one of the coolest cats in California, a dad of four, a spiritual man with a beautiful soul who found us on the internet.

He was the perfect Strategy Sprints coach. Although I don't require additional coaching certifications besides my Strategy Sprints certification, he was already a successful coach with a calendar of clients he served. He was attracted to my certification programme because he wanted to help clients get real, tangible results they can put in the bank. And he was wildly successful in his role.

Then, after three months, he sent me a video. He began, 'Simon, this isn't working…' and I was crushed, along with everyone on the team. Giorgio said he was leaving because we didn't have processes in place for our certified coaches. And that was true. We were building the processes as we went along. I decided never again would a great coach leave us because of our processes. The thing I wasn't doing was creating the onboarding flow like a railway for a train so the new hires could quickly get on track and stay the course.

So, I paused the hiring funnel to do the deep work of creating a Standard Operating Procedures (SOPs) manual for the coaches. I realized it wasn't for my employees to figure out how to perform their positions; as the CEO, I needed to lay that out for them. At some point, you must accept that you are alone as an entrepreneur and be of service. Instead of bothering your team if there's work to do on the weekend, it falls to you. And it is your job to create the SOP manual, not the job of the people in those positions. This holds true across industries and levels of responsibility, from engineers to baristas. If you don't know exactly what you're hiring this person to do all day so they achieve the KPIs, they won't know the most important tasks or the best way to go about things in your business. Leave it to them to figure out what to do all day and you'll have a lot more trial and error – as well as success that's hard to repeat – because there's not a playbook.

After I implemented the SOPs and many of the hiring processes in this chapter and the next one, I interviewed Sunil. He had managed the strategy practice for Ernst & Young for 25 years, and he wanted to pay six months in advance for a franchise licence with Strategy Sprints. A week later, Zack from Uber Eats came into our funnel for the same offer. If a business coach can pick a dream team, he'll want one coach who has seen a company scale, and then another one who's led an advisory practice. And for my coaching business, once the processes were in place, then these top coaches came. And they stayed. Without the processes, it's not likely I could have retained these A-Players.

In this chapter, I share the hiring tools I created so I didn't just find A-Players, but I also retained them for the long haul:

- Create the Job Scorecard.
- Write the Standard Operating Procedures manual.
- Build an inspiring landing page and application.

It was a big risk to invest my time and attention in the hiring system, and in the end, it has paid off. Most businesses focus on optimizing the hiring funnel and disqualifying applicants. But I find that the bigger problem is earlier in the funnel – how do we connect with our tribe? To find people like us, how do we help them see that we have shared values? A-Players expect good processes and will leave if they don't find them because they have the luxury of choice. They know that if they are expected to create your processes, they can create their own, and they may just leave and do so. However, when your hiring processes express your core values and you build the railway so your top talent will easily stay on track, you're in a much better position to attract and retain the highest-quality team members.

Create the job scorecard

When we start to feel short-staffed, we look at which tasks are taking big chunks of time and could be done by someone else. Our rule of thumb for when it's time to hire is the point at which a team member feels they could bring three times the value to the business if they could bring in a full- or part-time worker to take something off their plate so they can work on higher-value tasks. If we don't have this clarity, we can hire too soon and create a difficult situation of too much payroll overhead and not enough available work for this new person to do what is high enough value. That would be our fault, not theirs. However, with this certainty that an additional hire would create more opportunity for us, the first thing that we do before we decide to advertise a role is create a Job Scorecard.

The Job Scorecard is how we manage the performance of team members and discuss their performance over time. However, you should create this scorecard for a given job before you post an open position. This will assist with onboarding and managing your expectations and those of your new hires. Then, going forward, this scorecard allows you to review their progress on a monthly and quarterly basis. Check out the Strategy Sprints

Job Scorecard through the action tools link at the end of this chapter and download the template to follow along.

We begin the scorecard with a role overview that includes your vision for the role to be filled. This should include the most important KPI this person will be responsible for, where the number is now, where you want the number to go exactly, and by when. For example, 'This salesperson will be responsible for raising current conversion rates from 25 to 45 per cent in 90 days.' Or 'This SEO strategist will be responsible for increasing our visibility score from 20 to 45 per cent in 90 days.' This creates a very clear metric the new hire can use to measure their performance and where they should spend most of their time, which would be on sales calls. This is also possibly data you might use later when writing your job landing page, as I discuss later in this chapter.

With the vision for the role clear, then describe your A-Player definition for the person you will hire. Give some thought to the values this person will hold, what motivates them, what they are great at, and what it's like to work with them. Also, consider what your ideal hire's dreams and expectations are and flesh that out in the overview. In an ideal hiring situation, there's a perfect match with your A-Player definition and the applicant's dreams and expectations. When those things are not aligned between yourself and the applicant, there's unlikely to be a good fit. For example, because we're a remote company, our best employees desire to travel and want to be able to work from anywhere, and that's a dream we can help them realize. Our best team members are also deeply invested in getting our clients results and want to provide meaningful, tangible results, and if someone doesn't identify with that message, they probably won't be happy or successful on our team.

The scorecard also has a section for 'success' that you will leave blank for now. In the job interviews, when you find candidates that share your vision for the role and their expectations and dreams align with your A-Player description, take note of their responses in the 'success' field. Ask about the applicant's definition of personal and professional success, as well as how they will know if they are succeeding in this role. Take careful notes and consider if their answers fit your business's culture and the role. You can also refer to these answers later in performance reviews to see if they are meeting their own standards for success and if not, why, and offer solutions.

Next, list the three to five core skills you require for this position. It's commonly suggested to list software you want people to be familiar with or certifications and training they should have in the skills section. But those are skills that can be learned and taught. Not only that, but these skills can become obsolete and outdated quickly. I encountered this first-hand when I worked with a master public speaker and gained the skill of communicating with gravitas in an auditorium full of people. Then, because of the Covid-19 pandemic, I had to record my TEDx talk in a room with no one present, looking into a tiny camera with the light in my face. The skills didn't match my conditions, but fortunately I had something else, the skill of curiosity, and I found help for speaking on camera. I encourage you to think about what skills your A-Player will have that can't be taught. For me, those are things like an entrepreneurial mindset, problem-solving, being cool under pressure, willingness to learn, etc.

Following the skills list is a chart where you list the responsibilities the new hire will undertake and categorize them by the department in your business where that task lives. Consider what task is a function of sales, marketing, finance, HR, or fulfilment? Then what are the top four responsibilities? What's the frequency of each of these activities? Is it something that you expect daily, weekly, monthly, quarterly, or something else? What's the time estimation of each task, and how do they compound? This is a very insightful process that will tell you if the title and department for the role make sense, the hours required, what teams this person will work with, etc. You will use these answers not only to describe the role in interviews, but also to write an accurate job landing page.

Also include your company values and be prepared to briefly describe what they mean to you in the interviews and ask applicants what those values mean to them. You will want these values to be present in the job description as well, which I discuss later in this chapter. Our values are focus, freedom, flow, humble, hungry, and happy. Having these clearly defined will differentiate you from the other opportunities when an A-Player is looking for the right place for their talent, and the values also deter applicants that aren't, for example, humble or are not generally happy.

Lastly, include the KPIs for this position. You begin the vision with one metric they are responsible for, and then include a few 90-day goals to be achieved within their first three months; these may include personal goals like a number of sales calls completed, as well as team goals like a total number of new clients. These goals should be measurable and specific, aiming for three numbers to hit for each goal. Also include when and how monthly and quarterly reviews will take place. This is a powerful way to set expectations and make sure they are clear between yourself and a new team member.

To create your first Job Scorecard, start with the first draft. It will change anyway every couple of weeks. It should do. It should be a living document like everything that is in the Sprints universe. Everything should be started quickly and kept as simple as possible because it is a living document that will change and evolve week by week and hire by hire as you learn.

Write the standard operating procedures

Let's say you want to delegate the whole hiring system so that you as a CEO can go on a four-week vacation to the beach or to the mountains or wherever you want to go with your friends and your family. What can you do? You must create SOPs so that everything you would do for hiring can be done by someone else. In the same way, if I want a new coach to do all the tasks that my most successful coaches complete, I must outline what those tasks are and how to complete them in the most excellent way. Then, any new coach can pick up the SOPs and see exactly what to do and how to do it, so they aren't making it up as they go along and instead learn from the best practices you and your team already learned from trial and error.

When we create an SOP for a new task or even an entirely new role or function, we use an approval checklist to make sure all the required elements are present:

- The vision of success for the role is discussed and clarified with the CEO and other key players.
- Version 1 is created to list all the tasks and steps to complete them.
- Version 1 is reviewed for first feedback by necessary stakeholders.
- A second version is created, benefiting from the feedback.
- Version 2 is finalized.
- Version 2 is set up in the project management system to fire task reminders automatically.
- The new SOP is adopted.
- Team recaps lessons learned and implements additional improvements for SOP.
- This SOP is complete.

To create meaningful SOPs, do not skip any steps in the checklist or do them out of order. If you skip the first discussion and instead ask a team member to write a draft of an SOP, it's possible that it will miss the mark because it's what they guess or assume you want. Or if this new hire wouldn't report to you, not including the leader or manager the person in this role would report to can also cause mistakes and waste time. Once a draft is completed, don't move to implement before poking holes in the ideas and looking for things to add or improve, as well as removing redundancies. Also, once the new task is set up, the job here isn't over until those performing the role provide feedback and there may be continued optimization before a new best practice is fully realized and becomes a complete SOP.

For example, when we first decided to add Instagram as a lead-generating platform, none of us had experience in that arena, and it might have seemed like a good time to hire someone. But what could we ask them to do, exactly? How could we hold them accountable? What metrics would be reasonable and doable? We needed to walk the walk and learn what would be required through our own trial and error with creating posts and writing the copy, engagement strategies, etc. Then we had the tools to write the SOP and were able to bring in the right person who could learn this platform instead of having our hands tied to rely on an expensive consultant or marketing agency when we were still testing the viability of that platform as a fit or not for our marketing efforts.

I hope this inspires you to start handing over processes and systems and training new hires or existing team members to complete any task with an SOP. You will want to have your SOPs fully prepared before onboarding a new team member so that as soon as they join, they will be presented with the SOPs and be empowered to successfully complete them with assistance from the project management system's reminders. This way, you also become less and less of a bottleneck for the organization by avoiding lengthy training periods.

When you have a team member who introduces a new task for themselves or innovates a better way to complete a task, have them add the new process to the SOP for their role. This is one example of how you can let your people start growing into the responsibilities of creating processes. And they will be helping you create that railway for the next person who assumes that task to stay on track.

Build an inspiring landing page and application

With your Job Scorecard and the SOPs created for the role you're hiring for, it's time to do what you probably thought would come first and create the landing page for your job advertisement. Even though you may post the job on third-party platforms and use other strategies I share in Chapter 13 to get the word out, there are many advantages to also creating a landing page on your website that conveys and collects information.

Be aware that with the job description on your website, this doubles as an opportunity to speak to potential customers and clients, as well as job applicants. So, it's important to talk about who you are, what you do, how easy it is to work with you, etc on this page. You're sharing your business's culture and showcasing how your team members get results for your clients. At the same time, you're revealing the inner workings of your business and how you get things done.

I like to create my job landing pages with simple design and copy, usually consisting of headlines, bullet points, and a short video that leads to an application page.

The headline message should focus on what is most important to your ideal A-Player, so if the position is in sales, most likely the sales numbers will be the biggest draw for them. Try to use the words your applicants use and the data that they're looking for, without industry jargon. In terms of data, yes it's sales numbers for a sales position, and for a marketing position, the attractive data might be the size of the budget. For an HR position, the data might be the employee retention numbers. If you are unsure what data and language will be most attractive for your desired applicants, check out *Words That Change Minds* by Shelle Rose Charvet (2019). This book was useful when I created my hiring pages because Charvet provides checklists for different kinds of people, their language patterns, and how to communicate with different people differently using Neurolinguistic Programming (NLP).

After your gripping headline, provide bullet points that outline the most important things the applicant needs to know for whether they are a fit for this role. Consider including the qualifications needed, like 'this is for you if you…'. Refer to your Job Scorecard if you have trouble finishing that sentence. The goal is to describe your A-Player, who they will work with and in what context, your expectations, what you stand for, and your next steps if they want to apply. As you edit and revise these bullets and create your video, really think about standing in the shoes of the person you want seeing this landing page and thinking, 'this is a perfect fit for me'. Empathize with them about what other things they've done in the past that got them this far but haven't taken them further, what they most desire and dream to do, and how this position can help them get there.

Your video is a chance for the potential applicants and customers to meet you and feel your energy. It may feel counterintuitive, but even though in the hiring process applicants are trying to sell themselves to you, you are also selling yourself to them. The video is a great chance to do just that. Be sure to introduce yourself and your mission and values. Address the listener as your target A-Player with all the qualities you're looking for and briefly review the information in the bullets because some people may click the video immediately and not read the bullets. You might also include closed captioning on the video so people can watch it with the sound off if they are at work or if they are hearing impaired. End the video with a clear call to action for people to click below and apply.

The call to action for 'Apply Now' should be a button that takes them to an application page. Our form begins with fields to input their name, email address, and location. After they submit these inputs, the next page shares that our company is remote, so you can live and work anywhere, a detail that is part of our core identity. For us, a person who lives in, say, Boston, and wants to work in Boston with local co-workers is the wrong lead to fill a remote role. We lead with location and that we are remote, so we don't waste each other's time in that case.

Then, we ask, 'what excites you the most about this role?' We want to know their passion and what is exciting about us to them, and we ask this question for every position – period. If their answers don't inspire us, that person is probably not the best fit, even if they have experience on paper. Here are some other questions we always include:

- How many hours are you interested in working?
- What are you doing now?
- Why do you think you are the best candidate?
- What could you bring to the table?

The answers to these questions tell us if it makes sense to invite the applicant to the next step of the hiring process, which I discuss in Chapter 13. Obviously, if they want more or fewer hours than are required, that's most likely a dealbreaker. What they are doing now gives us an indication of the context of their search – are they between jobs or looking to leave another role? The third question is interesting because humility is one of our core values, so a great answer for us to this question is about the team and working together, but this is also a chance for them to show that they are hungry and eager to succeed. The last question gives us an indication of how they might stand out against other excellent applicants. Maybe one person has an idea for a new marketing avenue we hadn't considered or another has contacts in a new industry we'd like to expand into. Those details matter.

We also ask for links to profiles on LinkedIn, Facebook, and Instagram. An applicant's social media presence is relevant to us because we are a very human-interaction-related service company. We work with humans on raising the humanity of their interactions to grow their business through technology. We want to work with people who are capable of interacting, which we can see in social profiles. We look at how they carry themselves, how they interact, and how many interaction points they have on average. That is very relevant information when you are screening for the best people.

Now think of your company's needs and what's necessary for your application process. What information do you want them to know before they accept a call? Like in our case, it is that we are a remote team. Also, what do you want to know about applicants before you jump on the call with them? Include any items that are your dealbreakers.

The last thing to create for your hiring page is an automatic response applicants will get after they complete this first stage of the application process. This generic email should thank them for applying and let them know what the next step will be if they are invited to continue the process, as well as when to check back if they don't hear from you and when they should expect a response. These details can prevent applicants from sending emails asking if the application was received or when they will find out the result. Also, this means you must have some idea of your own deadlines. How long will you keep the position open? What turnaround time is reasonable to send qualified applicants to the next stage? Consider who is involved in the screening process. It may be useful for you to create an SOP for screening applicants and delegate the first round of screening to a qualified team member. In other cases, especially if the role is sensitive, you may want to look at the first round of applicants yourself.

Final thoughts

Doing the necessary planning with your Job Scorecard and SOP saves time in the long run, not only with what to write or include on your job landing page and application, but also so you hire and successfully onboard the right people to retain them in the long run. These activities also help you avoid hiring too early when the role isn't clearly defined and it would be difficult to bring someone in and measure their work or hold them accountable. Your inspiring landing page and applications will then be beacons to your ideal candidates that they have finally found the work they've been looking for, because they share your values and want to be a part of your company's culture. For job seekers that aren't a fit, they may see this for themselves and not enter your job funnel at all, which is a win-win. Not to mention that potential clients may also see this information and consider it a selling point for why to work with you because of what you stand for and how you support your team of A-Players. In the next chapter, I share how to drive viewers to the application page and what happens next with people who pass the first stage of the application process all the way to a signed contract.

ACTION TOOLS

strategysprints.com/tools

CHAPTER THIRTEEN

Hiring simplified

When you hire suppliers, you'll want to go through a similar process to what I outlined for hiring in the last chapter, including creating a job description with KPIs and SOPs for the tasks involved. But that's not all. It's important to take them through an interview process like the one I share in this chapter to make sure the supplier or new hire is a perfect fit.

I learned this lesson the hard way and lost time and money because I went with the wrong agency once. They were technically the right agency according to their reviews, and they had the necessary skills. So, I did my homework. But, in working together I was frustrated with the weekly progress reports that didn't include any problem-solving and wanted to strangle them over Zoom. At the end of a three-month trial, I got a partial refund.

In retrospect, I had made the decision to go with that agency because of their price, which was the best deal I was quoted for the work. Price shouldn't be the deciding factor. Instead of the cheapest, now when I choose suppliers and team members, I look for if they get what we stand for. They must bring extra knowledge and see things I don't see – and have the guts to say it. They also need to care enough to improve what we're working on together when a project isn't going well. This is about having shared values and actually caring about our mission.

Now, with the new agency, I prepare for the weekly meetings two days in advance and am excited with new ideas to share. This agency is more expensive, but we have true collaboration, and that's how a good project should go. When this is your standard of measure, a hire you make may not feel technically right, but it will feel right at gut level. You'll know in your stomach if you have a good collaboration and are curious what they will say and how they will react… With this collaboration, your suppliers also become referral partners for other key hires and great customers because they will share your filter.

On a deeper level, the common belief is that work should be formal, painful, and we are happy when it's over. Usually, that's the attitude towards suppliers, but I want to create something different. What if these relationships aren't painful or draining? It can be blissful and joyful when you embrace the roller coaster. There is nothing golden at the end when you exit the ride, there's just a roller coaster as you build your village as a vibrant ecosystem.

Many times, I'm drained after a heavy week, and I crawl into a meeting and want to stop a project. And then my team or the suppliers remind me that I inspired them to try a new solution, and the purpose and energy come back to me. I re-animate the dream for myself. Surround yourself with those who share your mission, and your leadership can create momentum even when you're not present.

One thing I've noticed in my own hiring pipeline and have seen in the larger professional area is that for employees, output and purpose are becoming more important. Employees like to know their work has meaning, so the hiring strategies I share in this chapter accomplish two things. You demonstrate to your A-Players that they will play meaningful roles in a mission they care about, and you find people who will not just be worker bees, but partner with you. These strategies include:

- Social outreach with hiring copy to make it clear what you stand for and your mission that will attract people who share your values.
- Three tests to see how the interviewee responds to pressure and rises to challenges.
- Interviews to get a sense of their energy and build rapport.
- Trial, offer, or rejection so you both prove to each other this is a great fit before the position is permanent.
- Hiring system checklist to delegate tasks and automate everything.

It's true that it can take two weeks of steady work to get all these elements into place, and then your hiring system will run like a machine with very little additional work. This is a final, important piece of your freedom as the CEO so hiring procedures don't eat away at your time and you're not starting over from nothing every time you need a new team member. This predictable hiring pipeline will support your growth strategies as you continue to scale your business.

Social outreach with hiring copy

From the last chapter, you created your hiring landing page and application. Now, the goal is to drive the right people to that page. In this case, you write hiring copy to share in social media posts and emails, but don't forget that these pieces of writing also serve as marketing. Just as your job landing page might be seen by potential clients, the same applies here.

The first outreach we do when we have a hiring page ready to accept applications is to write to our email list and other strategic partners to ask, 'Hey, we are searching for this job candidate. Do you know the right person?' With this strategy, we get amazing referrals and raise awareness that we're growing. These emails and the hiring posts I describe in this section also generate a ton of client conversations. They might get excited to find that I have a coach in the country where they are. Money attracts money, and impact attracts impact, and your job announcement is an invitation for people to join the party you show to be in progress. The interest you create is like what happens when you pass by a restaurant and smell amazing food cooking in the kitchen. The people in the kitchen are clearly ready to serve you a delicious meal. Other people are already eating inside. You, the customer, must join them and walk through the door.

Although we begin with emailing our list of raving fans, we primarily attract applicants through posting on our social media channels – Facebook, LinkedIn, and Instagram. In fact, 80 per cent of our hiring happens over social media. So, how do you create raving fan-level buzz amidst the noise of social medial? To create this magnetism in your hiring copy, you once more think about your positioning and what makes you unique. This is your chance to show who you really are and let others touch the magic. It should be written in your language and displayed with the colour, style and emotion you want to convey. Include your 30-Second Pitch or other compelling marketing assets you created in Chapter 11 that show your positioning. For us, we say they are going to work with entrepreneurs to help them save time and grow their business. That is basically what our hires really need to be passionate about if they want to work with us on our mission.

The same as any piece of social media copy, you'll start with a hook. Here's one I posted on Facebook for a marketing position: 'Hey, we're hiring a marketing lead ninja.' This works on several levels. If you are a marketing ninja, I'm speaking your language. If you are timid about marketing and think of yourself as more of a marketing white belt, this isn't for you. The language is polarizing and very Strategy Sprints™. And for a potential customer who wants to know if my business can deliver, I just told you I've got a marketing ninja on my payroll. Quite compelling evidence that our team can support your marketing efforts. The rest of that post briefly highlighted the benefits, expectations, and a call to action to enter the application process.

Here's another example of a social media hook for a project manager role: 'Project Managers, your dream is ___. You fill in that blank.' The language in this copy perfectly fits our values because the person who wants to fill in this blank has dreams they can fulfil with us. They want to supply a piece of the vision and not just be told what to do. Those people without defined dreams who don't want to be creative will keep scrolling. And for the ideal clients, to see the freedom and collaboration we create with our star players, when they share this collaborative approach, they know we are a good fit.

I've also seen hiring copy be successful in driving the right applicants with more direct hooks such as 'To all candidates…' and then listing the detailed skills we're looking for. Providing those details also repels applicants who know they don't measure up. We also had a good response with 'Who's the smartest person you know? Let them apply for this job'. This hook creates curiosity, but only for people who are quite smart themselves or know a very clever person who is job hunting. These examples are also signals to potential clients that tell them what kind of A-Players they're going to work with when they hire your company.

Be honest with your expectations and be very clear about what is important to you. The most important thing is to write directly to the people you want to interview. Create some hiring copy, review it with your team, and post it. See the responses you get and continue refining to find the right message that will bring you fabulous team members.

You might have heard that industry norms suggest interviewing 200 applicants, but that's often not reasonable for a small business. With this very specific hiring funnel, we look for about 40 great candidates to interview. If we don't get a good pool of applications from the hiring posts, we also send emails to possible applicants in our database to inform them that there are available positions in the company. These might be people we interviewed and liked, but they weren't a perfect fit for a role. Or they might have inquired at a time when we didn't have an opening for their skill set.

Then if an email campaign doesn't bring enough applications, we also reach out on traditional platforms with the job posting. In the past, we've had good results with AngelList, Craigslist, TechCrunch, SmartRecruiters, and ZipRecruiter. Using these platforms, which are mostly free, is as easy as creating a corporate account and posting your hiring ad. Angellist and TechCrunch have sent us the highest-quality applications, but test what's going to be best for your needs.

Three tests

At three different stages in the application process, I give the applicants a test. The first test is a demo task, which tells me about a person's skill level and attitude. Next, successful applicants are invited to complete a behaviour test. The next test comes after the 20-minute interview and before the longer interview. At each stage of the tests, I'm looking for the top candidates to rise to the top and impress me. Below I go into detail about how to create each of these tests and automate them.

First demo test

A hiring manager with a major tech start-up and I were discussing our hiring tests casually once as we were waiting to be interviewed in a panel discussion. He shared that for applicants who want to be coders with their company, the application process includes a live demo or hiring test. In the interview, they ask the applicant to share the screen and create some lines of code right then. I like this approach because the best way to know how someone will perform in a role is to tailor the demo to the task they will perform if hired. In many interviews, applicants are presented with an abstract problem and asked to solve it. Instead, I like to have them do the real work in real time. The best demo task is on or near the job because then I can see if they lack information, how they deal with setbacks, and how they deal with frustration and uncertainty.

Here's how this works for when we have a position we want to fill. First, think through the job position to determine what could be a small, incremental task that they can do to show they have the right skills, know-how, and are willing to do the work. We automate an email with this hiring task and send it to all our applicants within three hours of receiving their application. If we don't know how they will complete this task, then from an application alone, we don't know yet if we want to interview them or not. You must design a test for each position one time, and then automate the delivery for any time you are advertising this role again.

For instance, when we have a sales position to fill, the task we assign is to review a video of me doing a sales call and then create a video giving me feedback on the call. We specifically ask them to comment on:

- What do you think Simon did well?
- What could he improve?
- Which question do you like?
- What could he have done differently?

They create a short video, and we can see how they are in person, how they relate, how they speak, how they carry themselves, and how we like their ideas and if they 'get' us. This is a meaningful task exactly related to the job role. Don't give a generic type of task like calculating how many XYZ there are in China, which I have seen other companies do in their hiring processes. These generic tasks that aren't related to the role waste everyone's time, which says something about your own professional standards and processes – a lot of excess busy work.

Some applicants will never complete the task, so goodbye. Others will do one of two things. They will create a video, or they will reply with an excuse or question. Look for the applicant to either share excuses or display ownership in the demo test. If there are excuses, that's a red flag because they're not dealing proactively when they don't know something. They might lack motivation or ability. Whereas if they take responsibility for what doesn't work and ask questions, that's a sign they may be trainable. Even better if they simply create the video and you love their energy and feedback, but allow those who ask questions to get answers and then complete the task.

Behaviour test

It is customary in the job application process to have everyone complete a personality test. I don't find that helpful because the indexes are judgements that are independent of the business context. Consider that in the context of parenting, you will have one pattern of communication with your children, maybe even different for each child. And then in the context of co-workers, your communication patterns are likely quite different. That's why context is key.

I prefer behavioural context-specific analysis, which considers the business context. A great example of this approach is the LAB Profile® created by Shelle Rose Charvet (I recommend her book in the previous chapter). At the time of writing this book is still a free online tool you can send applicants to complete and share their results. Another behaviour test we appreciate is the Kolby Test, which is inexpensive but does charge a fee for use. With both tests, test takers select the context, which is role specific. So, instead of even a generic 'business' context, the test tailors to a 'sales' context or 'human resources' context. Then, the questions generate specifically for the strengths and traits desirable for that context.

After the applicant completes the test, they get an automated email that thanks them for this information and lets them know what will happen next. If they move forward, the next step is a 20-minute interview, which I discuss in the Interviews section of this chapter.

Professional process test

After the 20-minute interview, the next stage of your hiring funnel is the professional process test, which you can administer entirely through email automation. Have the test automated to send to the people you want to know more about from your interviews. This second test should only be offered to the top people you interviewed and were impressed with. I have seen many firms that make this second test difficult in the form of a case study to solve or a riddle. The thing is, that pointless exercise shows how low the standard of your precision is. Ouch. Don't do that. Instead, conduct a professional process test that shows what your processes are and measures if the candidates understand and can implement the process. So, give a controller a controlling task, a salesperson a sales task, etc.

For the second test for sales applicants, we share an informational video about our 90-Day Programme. Then, we present them with a prospective client, Andy, who wants to know if this offer is a good fit for him. The problem is, he makes $15K/month now, and that number is sporadic and volatile. He wants to increase to $25K/month in a reliable way. Then, we ask the applicant to create a three-minute video and share what they would say to Andy about the 90-Day programme. This test is invaluable.

Job seekers can tell you that they were the best salesperson at Coca-Cola Asia Pacific. Yes, maybe, but you will see if they can sell your offer when they do a three-minute video. You'll discover how they carry themselves, the level of their professionalism, their preparations, their delivery. You will see all that in three minutes. This test tells you more than the CV line that they were the best salesperson anywhere.

We also observe what, if any, questions they ask and how fast they shift when they get an answer. Of course, we're Sprinters, so speed is one of the things that are appropriate and important in our world. We also check how fast they send the video and how many excuses happen along the way. Those few who successfully complete the professional process test should get an additional email for a second, longer hiring interview. More about that in the next section of this chapter.

Interviews

I conduct interviews at two points of the hiring funnel. After the behaviour test, we have this analysis, the outcomes of the demo, and their application. All this information helps us choose the people that warrant a 20-minute interview. This should happen with a person instrumental in the hiring decision, so often that might be yourself, a chief executive, or a manager. After this interview, you send the highest-scoring applicants to the professional process test I discuss in the previous section of this chapter. And for the people who ace that test, we give a final 30-minute interview to gather additional information and make decisions about who moves on to a trial phase.

Those who move forward after the behaviour test and first demo test are sent an invitation to schedule a first 20-minute interview. This email can be automated, and ours includes a scheduling link via Calendly. At this point, most of the preparation for this interview is already done with your Job Scorecard from Chapter 12. During the conversation, you are looking for strengths, weaknesses, opportunities, risks, and additional information. To create these interview questions, we worked with a consulting firm that recommends *Topgrading (How to Hire, Coach, and Keep A Players)* (2005) by Bradford D Smart if you want more background on this process. Find the complete interview questions checklist available through the action tools link at the end of this chapter.

The first thing we cover in this call are the KPIs for this role from the Job Scorecard. Before I go over the KPIs, I set the stage to establish that at any point if I detect a dealbreaker, I will cut the meeting short, and if they find a dealbreaker, I encourage them to end the meeting early, too, so we don't waste each other's time. With this established, carefully explain the four or five measurable expectations, and for each one, take stock of the interviewee's verbal and nonverbal communication. As you'll see in our template, we then ask about their education, work experience, job-specific experience, dreams and aspirations.

After the interview, compile a short summary from the Job Scorecard and KPIs. Based on their experience and their reactions in the call, rate them from 1–5 on how likely it is they know how to do the work and how much they want to do it. We also like to document what we notice as strengths, weaknesses, opportunities, risks of the applicant, and the other notes. For example, if an applicant has been featured in 'Forbes under 30', that is interesting and relevant information that we also want to convey in the documentation.

The 30-minute interview follows a unique flow for each applicant depending on the role and our questions for them based on their test performances and follow-up questions about themselves. We set the agenda for the meeting based on these questions and how we like the answers. For example, if the person gave a great performance in the video and we thought they had good points, but they overlooked something we expected to hear, we might ask what they think about including that element. And if we learned something from them in the video, we might want to find out more about how they arrived at that idea. We also leave time on this call for them to ask additional questions because they are also interviewing us and deciding if this job is for them. At the end of this call, we let them know when to expect to hear from us to invite them for a 60-day trial if we decide to make that offer.

After the 30-minute interviews are conducted, decide who you want to offer a trial to. In your CRM, create a polite rejection thanking them for their time, letting them know you're going forward with someone else, and send it to everyone who is not moving forward. You should be able to write this once and then use the template for all the positions you hire for. Send an onboarding email to the winning candidate that outlines their next steps to officially joining your team in this role for a 60-day trial. Include a contract form for the trial and a non-disclosure agreement (NDA) to protect your intellectual property and client contact list. Additional onboarding items might include access to a dashboard of training materials and the SOPs, software logins they might need, invitations to standing meetings, scheduling a meeting within a certain timeframe, etc.

Trial, offer, or rejection

When you use our screening methods, from the job listing and job scorecard through the interviews and video tests, you will find that only the highest-quality applicants will make it to the trial. There are a lot of reasons the 60-day trial works best for Strategy Sprints™, although the shortness of our trial is often surprising to business owners with a corporate background. In that setting, trials tend to last at least three months, if not half a year or even an entire year. For industries that move more slowly than our online business, a longer trial might make more sense.

We have found that 60 days is plenty of time to work with someone and encounter stressful events with them to see how they react under pressure. When there's a problem or issue, how they handle it tells us if we want to work with that person for the long term or not. Do they still display our core values when they are disappointed or if they or someone else made a mistake? If we don't hit our goals, do they have ideas or just complain? To respect everyone's time, it's best to choose a trial period that is long enough that you will encounter the roller coaster of business and navigate it together and no longer than that.

In addition, during the trial period, we continue advertising for the position and bringing additional people through the hiring process. We keep interviewing because then redundancies are in place, and we minimize our risk during the trial. With the high turnover reality of the job market, we don't want to be surprised if someone drops out of the trial or quits just after it ends, as well as when we see that we don't have a good fit and decline to offer them the permanent position.

During the trial period, the applicant performs their tasks almost immediately because they have proved they know how to do the job, and they have the SOPs to follow. Only an agile business can operate this way. Digital companies need everyone on payroll to be producing, so we prepare the new hire in the hiring process, and from day one, they are completing tasks that align with their KPI goals. Bloating this process by making the new hire have a meeting with each member of the team, or sit through long videos about the company, etc is a waste of everyone's time and valuable payroll.

After 60 days the trial ends, and we review the applicant's performance and results. We discuss moments of challenge and how the applicant handled themselves, as well as where their numbers are. With these factors, we determine if the candidate will proceed to be invited to the position full time or not. A successful hire will have wowed us under pressure and come up with creative solutions and remained positive. Also, they will be making progress towards the 90-day goal. So, with the example of bringing sales conversions from 25 to 45 per cent, we would want them at least near or above 35 per cent to be making good progress. When these elements align, we have an A-Player and invite them to join the team.

If the trial reveals that someone wasn't a good fit, we let them go. This happens when it turns out they didn't share our values and complained a lot or weren't able to rise to the occasion during a challenge. In almost every case, when they didn't perform like an A-Player in a crisis moment, they're also not where we want them to be with progress on KPIs. You must be the best of the best to meet our standards, and to perform our tasks to excellent completion and grow the business, it takes top performance even under pressure.

In many cases, people who are not a fit can see this disconnect for themselves already and may put in their notice first. They will know if their numbers are low and that you are holding them accountable for those KPIs. Sometimes it's a gift if they see the bad fit too and leave, because after all, you are still interviewing people for the role and can offer the trial to the next person who might be a better fit. And when you have the conversation to let them go, you have the report with their numbers that are not what they have to be for the role.

For those to whom you offer the full-time role, now send a hiring contract. Your contract should also be in your CRM and ready to go. Our contracts describe services and payments, terms, termination, confidentiality, indemnification, etc. If your business is global, be sure to seek legal counsel for international laws and standards, as well as those applying to your state and country. Congratulations! You now have an excellent team member to bring value to your business and fulfil their dreams in the process.

Hiring system checklist

Now let's review the nitty-gritty of the technicalities of how you create a system out of your hiring pipeline. While describing the hiring system in this chapter and the previous one, I mention emails you can write once and then plug into your CRM and send automatically in some cases, or with a click of a button in others.

Our hiring system is created in Asana, which is a project management system. Here is a checklist of hiring assets and automations to create to follow our example:

- Job Scorecard
- SOPs
- Hiring landing page and application
- Application received email
- Hiring copy for social outreach
- Demo test invitation email
- Demo test
- Demo test pass/fail reply
- Behaviour test invitation email
- Behaviour test
- Behaviour test pass/fail reply
- 20-minute interview invitation email
- 20-minute interview
- Post interview pass/fail email
- Professional process test invitation
- Professional process test
- Post-test pass/fail email
- 30-minute interview invitation email
- 30-minute interview
- Trial offer onboarding email/ rejection email
- Onboarding materials
- NDA
- 60-day trial contract
- 60-day trial
- Post-trial rejection
- Hiring contract offer

Without this checklist, if you have 300 people coming into your hiring funnel every week, that volume would be overwhelming for a non-systematized business. With this hiring system it is easy to manage such a volume and it can be done by one executive assistant because there is so much automation. This means you can be on a long vacation and still have a pipeline of applicants coming in, and they're having a great onboarding experience that conveys what it is to work with you and what is important to you.

This freedom gives you the possibility to find worthy and trusted people and filter them from the long list of applicants in the top of the hiring funnel to the shortlist where world-class people rise to the top, join your team, and make your vision happen. Start a process like this one and improve it every week.

Final thoughts

When you write hiring copy for social posts and emails, and keep in mind that you're also talking to your clients, this writing also functions as marketing copy. You write your hooks so powerfully that your most ideal candidate identifies with the call instantly, and your best customer is thrilled to see this level of excellence required of your team members. The demo test and professional process test give you two opportunities to see the candidates on camera and feel their energy and measure their performance. At the same time, their ability to deal with challenges will reveal their character. You see even deeper into their mindset with the behaviour test that offers contextual questions based on the role, so the personality type data is useful to see if that person is a fit with your company's values. The interviews are mostly done for you with the Job Scorecard and your additional notes so you can sit back and listen to your gut on how they respond to you and your feelings about them. Offer a trial such as 60 days to test the relationship and see how you do together in moments of pressure. When their performance and KPIs are excellent, make the hire, and when that's not the case, keep working your hiring system to find the right candidate who is probably somewhere along your checklist right now. With your automations in place for all the email correspondence, much of this system can be automated so you have more freedom to do the growth projects on your list and enjoy your happy life.

ACTION TOOLS

strategysprints.com/tools

Appendix 1: A note to you, the reader

My mission in life is to help sprinters realize their dream. Sprinters are the people who build more than they talk. The creators.

Being a creator is lonely. At times it's overwhelming. But it does not have to be like that.

We have come so far together. Happy to coach you from here, in real life.

Take your first step by booking a demo call with me: www.strategysprints.com

Let's scale your business faster than ever!

Simon Severino

Appendix 2: YOUR GAME PLAN

There are so many moving parts in running a business.

Wondering what to fix next?

Spend 8 minutes to identify your bottleneck

Our quick game plan helped:

- BI Consultant: Double sales in 3 months with a better CRM flow.
- Insurance Broker: Triple enquiries with our marketing blueprints.
- Financial Advisor: Onboard clients faster = 65% shorter sales.
- Business Coach: Get gross margin from 21% to 78% in 12 weeks.

Get YOUR quick gameplan here: www.strategysprints.com

Index

NB: page numbers in *italic* indicate figures or tables

7-Second Tagline 137–38
30-Second Pitch 136–37, 159
80% Ready Page, the 91–93, 102, 107, 132
   objections, handling 92, 98
   social proof 92
   trust, building 92–93
90-Day Growth Plan, creating a 38–46
   Goals 40–42
   Growth KPIs 44–46, *45*, 115
   Positioning 42–44
   Vision / Main Theme 39–40, *40*

Abdaal, Ali 14
advertising 4, 130
   Customer Acquisition Cost (CAC) 130
   Facebook Ads 88, 121
      retargeting ads 122, 130
   Instagram ads 122, 130
   jobs 159–61
   and storytelling 21–22, 25
   YouTube ads 89
   see also marketing
affiliate partnerships 47–48
agile companies 49, *49*
Alibaba 17
Allen, David 63, 65
Amazon 140
AngelList 161
Apple 9
   growth, benchmarking 119
   'Lisa Campaign, The' 21–22, 25
   'Think different' 22
artificial intelligence (AI) 10, 111
Asana 70, 71, 168
Ashby, Ross 84
assets, your 135–44
   7-Second Tagline 137–38
   30-Second Pitch 136–37, 159
   authority content 141–42, 143
   phrase, your 139–40
   platform, professional 142–43
   social proof 140–41
   uniqueness, your 138–39
audience targeting 11–15
authority content 4, 141–42, 143
avatar, your ideal 4, 14, 42–43, 86, 100

Bain & Company 116
behavioural test 162–63
benchmarking 115
   industry benchmarking 119
   see also Key Performance Indicators (KPIs)
'big goal', your 17–18
Blue Ocean Strategy 8
blue ocean, the 8, 123, 135
brand ambassadors 116
Branson, Richard 22
Brown, Todd 130
burnout 75, 78
Burnt 143

Calendly 164
Calls to Action (CTAs) 125
cash flow 33
   see also sales, predictable
channels, choosing 123–24, 142–43
Charvet, Shelle Rose 152, 163
client, your ideal 12–14
Close.com 106
closing 109, 129
   Closing Day 76
   trial close (close-ended) 104
   trial close (open-ended) 103–04
Clubhouse 56
cold leads 107, 108
commodity model 85
complexity 65, 83
   Law of Requisite Complexity 84
complicatedness 83
confidence, building 15
content, reusable 124–25
Continuity Offer, your 85, 90–91
contract, offering a 167
Cooper, Bradley 143
Covid-19 pandemic 95, 149
Craigslist 161
CrossFit 140
Customer Acquisition Cost (CAC) 130
Customer Relationship Management (CRM) software
   choosing 106
   Discovery Calls, documenting 102
   Mail Chimp 140

INDEX

Customer Relationship Management (CRM) software (*Continued*)
  recruitment 165, 167, 168
  seven stages of 105–11, 112
    awareness 107–08
    closing 109
    continuity 111
    delivery 110
    nurturing 108
    sales opportunity, the 109
    upsell 110–11
  and your Value Ladder 4, 43

Daily Flow 63, 66–69, 67, 80
  number of items 67
  template 68
Daily Huddle 79
daily intentions 75–77
Data-Driven Dashboards 10
decision-making, streamlining your 47–60
  habits, productive 50, 51–59
    daily 51, 53–55, 63
    monthly 51, 53, 57–59
    weekly 51, 53, 56–57
  Strategy Sprints Compass 50–51, *51*, 51, 52, 57
definition of done (DoD) 64–65
demographics, limits of 13, 15
demo test 161–62
Discovery Calls 99–102
  documenting 102
  pre-call checks 101
  template for 100, 101
distractions, minimizing 71–72
Domino's Pizza 137

Einstein, Albert 22
email automation 126–29
  launch emails 127–29
  nurture emails 126–27
Employee Hiring and Onboarding Day 76
employee turnover 145–46
energy patterns, your 80–82
Equalizer Spreadsheet 10–11, *11*
Ernst & Young 146
Evernote 17
Eyal, Nir 67

Facebook 48
  Facebook Ads 88, 121
    retargeting ads 122, 130
  Facebook Groups 88, 89
  recruitment on 154, 159, 160
  reviews on 140

Farewell to Arms, A 12
feedback 58, 113–20
  feedback scores 115–16
    Neutrals 116, 119
    Superfans *116*, 116–17, 119
    Unsatisfieds 116, 117, 119
  industry benchmarking 119
  negative feedback 114–15
  Net Promoter Score (NPS) 44, 116, 117
  partnership, building 113–14, 118
  proactive, being 115
  response rates 113, 118
Five Levels of Business Fitness 3–5
Fulfilment Day 76
'full circle' 5

Gary-Vee Content Model 124
'Getting Things Done' (GTD) method 63, 80
Google 41
  Chrome 70
  Gmail Blocker 70, 71
  goal of 17
  Google Ads 88, 97–98
  Google calendar 75
  Messy Middle, The 127
  reviews on 140
growth plan, your 4, 33–46, 77
  90-Day Growth Plan, creating a 38–46
    Goals 40–42
    Growth KPIs 44–46, *45*, 115
    Positioning 42–44
    Vision / Main Theme 39–40, 40
  Growth Levers 34–38
    price / packaging 34–35
    productivity, exponential 37–38
    sales time / sales rate 35–36
    systematizing 36–37
'hustle', the 33

habits, productive 50, 51–59
  daily 51, 53–55, 63
  monthly 51, 53, 57–59
  weekly 51, 53, 56–57
Hemingway, Ernest 12
hiring 4, 145–69
  contract, offering a 167
  employee turnover 145–46
  hiring system checklist 167–68
  interviewing 164–66
  job application 153–54
    screening 154
    submission response 154
  job landing page 151–53
  Job Scorecard 145, 147–50, 164

Key Performance Indicators
(KPIs) 149, 165
person specification 148
responsibilities 149
skills, core 148–49
success, defining 148
values, company 149
vision for the role 148
social outreach 159–61
Standard Operating Procedures (SOPs)
manual, creating a 146, 150–51
suppliers, working with 157–58
tests
behavioural test 162–63
demo test 161–62
professional process test 163–64
trial period, the 166–67
hiring system checklist 167–68
hot leads 4, 29, 107, 108, 109
How Champions Think 15
HubSpot 106
'hustle', the 33

'Ideal Week', your 74–82, 83
blocking out time 78–80
daily intentions 75–77
elements, plotting the 77–78
energy patterns, your 80–82
template 75, 79
visual, making it 75
IFTTT 108
'imposter syndrome' 59
inbox management 71
Indistractable 67
influencers, using 141
Instagram 151
as an infinity pool 70
recruitment on 154, 159
retargeting ads 122, 130
Integrations 10
interviewing 164–66
Introduction to Cybernetics, An 84

job applications 153–54
screening 154
submission response 154
job landing page 151–53
Job Scorecard 145, 147–50, 164
Key Performance Indicators (KPIs) 149,
165
person specification 148
responsibilities 149
skills, core 148–49
success, defining 148

values, company 149
vision for the role 148
Jobs, Steve 21–22
joint venture (JV) relationships 47–48

Karate Kid, The 29
Key Performance Indicators (KPIs) 41–42
Growth KPIs 44–46, 45, 115
ownership of 48, 148
when hiring 149
Kim, Chan and Mauborgne, Renee 8
King Jr, Martin Luther 22
Kolby Test 163

LAB Profile® 163
launch emails 127–29
Law of Requisite Complexity 84
channels, winning 88, 89, 98, 123–24
cold leads 107, 108
Customer Relationship Management
(CRM) software, your 106, 107
Facebook Ads 88, 121
retargeting ads 122, 130
hot leads 4, 29, 107, 108, 109
'hustle', the 33
Instagram ads 122, 130
referrals 111
upselling 110–11
warm leads 4, 29, 107, 108, 130
website, your 21
80% Ready Page, the 91–93, 102,
107, 132
YouTube ads 89
leads, generating 97, 107
LinkedIn 56, 88, 97, 125
recruitment on 154, 159
'Lisa Campaign, The' 21–22, 25
loss aversion 30

Mail Chimp 140
Main Product, defining your 4, 85–87, 89, 110
benefits of 87
criteria for 86
pricing 86–87
Main Upsell, your 85, 89–90, 110
marketing 4, 121–33
assets, your 135–44
7-Second Tagline 137–38
30-Second Pitch 136–37, 159
authority content 141–42, 143
phrase, your 139–40
platform, professional 142–43
social proof 140–41
uniqueness, your 138–39

marketing (*Continued*)
    content, reusable 124–25
    email automation 126–29
        launch emails 127–29
        nurture emails 126–27
    mechanism, unique 130–31
    offer, irresistible 131–32
    positioning 122–23
    retargeting ads 130
    traction channels 123–24
Marketing Day 76
mechanism, unique 130–31
Messy Middle, The 127
'me time' 78, 80, 81
micro-commitment, triggering 88
milestones, celebrating 65–66
mindset, importance of 58–59
Minimalists, The: Less is Now 49
mission statements 16, 19
Momentum 70–71
Musk, Elon 31

Netflix 49
Net Promoter Score (NPS) 44, 116, 117
Neurolinguistic Programming (NLP) 152
nurture emails 126–27

objections, handling 104, 105, 129
    80% Ready Page, the 92, 98
    common objections 129, 132
    'vanilla', being 9
offer, irresistible 131–32
Osbourne, Ozzy 13, 24
owned channels 142

Pixar 22
positioning 122–23
Prince Charles 13, 24
priorities, importance of 74
productivity
    and burnout 75, 78
    as a growth lever 37–38
    habits, productive 50, 51–59
        daily 51, 53–55, 63
        monthly 51, 53, 57–59
        weekly 51, 53, 56–57
    see also time management, effective
professional process test 163–64
Project List 62, 63–66, 67
    definition of done (DoD) 64–65
    milestones, celebrating 65–66
    personal vs business projects 65
Protection Systems 63, 70–72, 71

distractions, minimizing 71–72
    'zone of genius' 70
PTYA: Part-Time YouTuber Academy 14
Public Relations Day 76
purpose *see* traction, creating

referrals 111
Reichheld, Fred 116
retargeting ads 130
Rolex 84
Rotella, Bob 15

Sales Day 76, 79
salespeople, hiring *see* hiring
sales, predictable 95–112
    Covid-19 pandemic, effect of 95–96
    Customer Relationship Management
        (CRM) 105–11, 112
        awareness 107–08
        closing 109
        continuity 111
        delivery 110
        nurturing 108
        sales opportunity, the 109
        upsell 110–11
    Discovery Calls 99–102
        documenting 102
        pre-call checks 101
        template for 100, 101
    following up 111–12
    objections, common 105
    Sales Estimation Number 98–99
    sales scripts, effective
        agenda 102–03
        benefits of 103
        close 104
        contrast 103
        deliverables 104
        next steps 104–05
        objection handling 104
        proposal 104
        qualify and diagnose 103
        trial close (close-ended) 104
        trial close (open-ended) 103–04
    sales tracking 95, 97–98, 99
Sample, describing the 85, 87–88
    micro-commitment, triggering 88
Scrum 64
Siemens 9
Skillshare 14, 125
Skywalker, Luke 24, 27
Slack 70, 71
Smart, Bradford D 164

SmartRecruiters 161
Snyder, Steve 22
social media 4; *see also* Facebook; Instagram; LinkedIn; YouTube
social proof 125, 132, 140–41
    80% Ready Page, the 91
    influencers 141
    media placement 141
SpaceX 17
'Sprinters', defining 1
Standard Operating Procedures (SOPs) 54
    Standard Operating Procedures manual, creating a 146, 150–51
Star Wars: A New Hope 24, 27
storytelling, elements of 22
    call to action (CTA), your 28–29
    hero, defining the 23–24
    hero's journey, the 26
    mission, defining the 24
    plan / solution, the 28
    success, describing 29–30
    transformation, mapping 30–31
    villain, picking a 24–28
Strategic Partnerships Day 76
Strategy Sprints Compass 50–51, *51*, 51, 52, 57
'superpowers', your 19
suppliers, working with 157–58
Sutherland, Jeff 64

Team Day 76, 79
TechCrunch 161
TEDx talks 7, 93, 149
Tesla 9, 17, 31
testimonials *see* social proof
tests (hiring)
    behavioural test 162–63
    demo test 161–62
    professional process test 163–64
'Think different' 22
Time Finder 53–54, *54*
time management, effective 61–72
    Daily Flow 63, 66–69, 67, 80
        number of items 67
        template 68
    Project List 62, 63–66, 67
        definition of done (DoD) 64–65
        milestones, celebrating 65–66
        personal vs business projects 65
    Protection Systems 63, 70–72, *71*
        distractions, minimizing 71–72
        'zone of genius' 70

Topgrading (How to Hire, Coach, and Keep A Players) 164
traction channels 123–24
'traction', creating 73–82
    'Ideal Week', your 74–82, 83
    blocking out time 78–80
    daily intentions 75–77
    elements, plotting the 77–78
    energy patterns, your 80–82
    template 75, 79
    visual, making it 75
    priorities, importance of 74
trial period, the 166–67
triggers, purchase 127
Tversky, Amos and Kahneman, Daniel 30

Uber Eats 146
Ultimate Question, The: Driving good profits and true growth 116
unique, being 8
upselling 110–11

Value Ladder 4, 43, 83–93, 106, 107
    80% Ready Page, the 91–93, 102, 107, 132
        objections, handling 92, 98
        social proof 92
        trust, building 92–93
    Continuity Offer, your 85, 90–91
    defining 84
    Main Product, defining your 85–87, 89, 110
        benefits of 87
        criteria for 86
        pricing 86–87
    Main Upsell, your 85, 89–90, 110
    Sample, describing the 85, 87–88
        micro-commitment, triggering 88
    Winning Channels 85, 88–89
'vanilla', being 7–8, 9, 123
Vaynerchuk, Gary 124
Verizon 138
vision, embodying your 16–20

wakeboarding 121–22
warm leads 4, 29, 107, 108, 130
website, your 4, 21–32
    challenges of 21
    storytelling, elements of 22
        call to action (CTA), your 28–29
        hero, defining the 23–24
        hero's journey, the 26

website, your (*Continued*)
    mission, defining the 24
    plan / solution, the 28
    success, describing 29–30
    transformation, mapping 30–31
    villain, picking a 24–28
Winning Channels 85, 88–89
Words That Change Minds 152

Yelp 140

Your Game Plan Audit 5
YouTube 35–36, 88, 91, 125
    Abdaal, Ali 14
    metrics on 124
    YouTube ads 89

Zapier 108
ZipRecruiter 161
'zone of genius' 70
Zoom 101, 158